Best of Majaz

Selection and English translation by

Kuldip Salil

Edited by

Om Sapra

rajpal

₹ 395
ISBN : 9789389373080
I[st] Edition : 2021, 3rd Reprint : 2025

BEST OF MAJAZ (Poetry)
(English translation of selected Urdu poetry of Majaz)
Selected and translated by Kuldip Salil
Printed at G.S. Offset, Delhi

RAJPAL & SONS
1590, Madarsa Road, Kashmere Gate, Delhi-110006
Phone : 011-23869812, 23865483, 23867791
e-mail : sales@rajpalpublishing.com
www.rajpalpublishing.com
www.facebook.com/rajpalandsons

Introduction

Two things have been common to a large number of Urdu poets-alcholism and unrequited love.

Starting with Meer and Ghalib and going on to Sahir and Majaz, these poets had a failed love affair which became a major source of their poetic outpourings.

It is not so among Hindi poets though there is a lot of love poetry in Hindi too.

In English, I can think of only two major poets who had an unrequited love affair. One was John Keats whose failed love for Fanny Brawne is well known. But even in Keats's case the failed relationship does not become a major source of his great poetry. The other is W. B. Yeats, whose love for Mand Gonne made Yeats almost mad. He waited till the age of fifty-one for Mand to say 'yes' to his marriage proposal. In Yeats's case failed love became a source of his major poetry.

Excessive drinking has been rampant among Urdu poets and has been the undoing of many of them. Jigar Muradabadi, Sahir Ludhianvi, Josh Malihabadi, Mirza Galib, Naresh Kumar Shaad, Adam and even Faiz Ahmed Faiz are the names that immediately come to mind in this context. Unfortunately, Majaz Lucknavi was a victim of both, unrequited love and alcoholism.

Asrar-ul-Haq Majaz Lucknavi was born in 1909, (some say 1911) in Radauli, Uttar Pradesh. His father Siraj-ul-Huq notwithstanding the fact that he was from a landed family, was the first person in Radauli who received higher education and took up a government job. Asrar thus, belonged to a family which while respecting old values of life aspired to be modern. And Majaz's extended family, as far as art and poetry go, is indeed very impressive. His sister, Safia, who married the noted poet Jaan Nisar Akhtar and is the mother of poet and lyricist Javed Akhtar.

Majaz received his early education in Lucknow and then moved to St. John College, Agra for higher studies. In Agra he met poets like Mueen Hasan Jazbi, Faani and Badauni and it was here that Majaz started writing poetry, the glow of which travelling through Aligarh and Delhi gradually spread in the entire country.

Majaz was so popular and his poetry such a rage that, according to the noted Urdu writer Ismat Chugtai, girls in the Women's College, Aligarh kept his poems under their pillows and drew lots with Majaz's name on them to find out who will marry him. They even thought of naming their sons after him.

Majaz completed his graduation from Aligarh Muslim University and moved to Delhi in 1936 where he got a job with All India Radio as the editor of their journal *Aawaz*. In Delhi, Majaz fell in love with a married woman from the higher strata of society. But this woman would not or could not reciprocate his love. He was heartbroken, left the job and Delhi and went back to Lucknow. It was in this dejected mood that he wrote 'Dilli Se Wapsi'

रुख़सते-दिल्ली तेरी महफ़िल से अब जाता हूं मैं
नौहागर जाता हूं मैं, नाला-ब-लब जाता हूं मैं

(I leave you Delhi, I leave your gatherings now
Mourning I leave, I leave weeping)

After leaving Delhi, Majaz worked for some time in the Bombay Information Service. Then alongwith Sardar Jafri and Sibte-Hasan, he edited a literary journal *Naya Adab*. Back in Delhi, he joined the Harding Library as Assistant Librarian. In the meantime his parents fixed his marriage. However when things were looking up for Majaz, perhaps learning about his drinking and wayward life, his marriage proposal was rejected.

This came as the proverbial last straw on the camel's back. As it had happened in the earlier love affair Majaz completely lost his mental balance. He took to heavy drinking and had a nervous breakdown. The girls who were at one time besotted with him were now afraid of marrying a mad man. His parents had thought that once he got married, he would settle down in life like a normal person. They had with great effort somehow restored his balance. But now the rejection of the proposal by the girl's father came as a bolt from the blue.

After the second breakdown, Majaz became a megalomaniac, telling people that he was the greatest poet after Ghalib and Iqbal. His family once again tried its best to bring him back to normal life, but to no avail. All his life, until his death in 1955, he remained an alcoholic. Sahir Ludhianvi who was himself a heavy drinker introduced Majaz in his journal *Savera* as a vagabond who was always drunk. This is the ruin that failed love affairs brought on him.

जिस दिन तुमसे नाता टूटा वारदात उस रात की है
तुमको था मालूम ये होगा, हैरत तो इस बात की है

(This misfortune occurred the day you snapped ties with me
And what is most shocking is that you knew it would happen)

In Majaz's drinking, his so called admirers and fans played no small a role. Besides being a poet Majaz was a great conversationalist. His fans and admirers would take him to their house or a tavern where they plied him with alcohol and enjoyed his brilliant conversation and recitation of poetry. It was at one such gathering that after getting him heavily drunk they left for their homes, leaving Majaz intoxicated on the terrace of the tavern where he froze to death in the freezimg winter night.

कुछ लोगों का करम है इसमें
कुछ साज़िश हालात की है!

(I am ruined partly by the so called kindness of the people and only partly my own circumstances.)

Majaz along with Jazbi, Josh, Faiz Ahmed Faiz, Sardar Jafri, Kaifi Azmi and Sahir among a large number of other Urdu writers belonged to the Progressive Writers Movement which sought to make poetry as an instrument of social change. During the 1930s and 1940s these poets were very popular. Social and political revolution was their credo. They wrote of a golden dawn when all disparities would be gone, exploitation of man by man, cruelties and injustice would cease to be, and there would be equal opportunities for everybody, love would be the defining characteristic of human heart and all discrimination due to religion and caste would end. The lilt and lyricism of some of the poets, Jigar Muradabadi for example, was most gripping. These poets were especially popular among the youth and Majaz was indeed a leading light among them. However, the partition of the country and the post-partition scenario dealt a huge blow to the idealism of these poets. Thus Faiz Ahmed Faiz wrote :

ये दाग़-दाग़ उजाला ये शब-गुज़ीदा सहर,
वो इन्तज़ार था जिसका ये वो सहर तो नहीं
ये वो सहर तो नहीं जिसकी आरज़ू लेकर
चले थे यार कि मिल जायेगी कहीं-न-कहीं

(This light all stained, this morning bitten by night
This is not the dawn we looked forward to
This is not the dawn we set out for
Hoping that we will find it somewhere somehow)

The riots and bloodshed after partition shocked everybody, especially the progressive writers and Majaz was no exception. In fact these developments aggravated his grief. He was further unhinged and took to still heavier drunking. Josh Malihabadi asked him to keep a watch while drinking :

घड़ी रख के पिया कर...

(Keep a watch beside you when you drink)

to which Majaz wittily but tragically replied :

मैं घड़ा रख के पीता हूं...

(I keep a pitcher (by my side) and drink.)

Majaz, like many other Urdu poets glorified drinking in his poetry. Adam wrote :

मैं मयकदे की राह से होकर गुज़र गया,
वरना सफ़र हयात का काफ़ी तबील था

(I passed via the tavern, otherwise
Life's journey would have been too long)

Mueen Hasan Jazbi's death came as a great shock to Majaz. One night, when drunk he was heard saying "Jazbi tu Urdu ka sab se bara shayer tha. (Jazbi you were the greatest Urdu poet)". There are reasons for Majaz saying so. Lives of both Majaz and Jazbi were rudderless and directionless. Pathos and drinking were common to both. Of course, Majaz is a greater poet than Jazbi, not that Jazbi is not a good poet. Majaz is a poet of social consciousness and, like Sahir, he revolts against constricting social customs. Although love is the recurring theme and an overriding passion in Majaz poetry, his intense opposition to social injustice is such that according to Asar Lukhnavi, a poet and critics, "Great Majaz was destroyed and mauled by conservative wolves."

Asar Lukhnavi also said that a Keats was born in Urdu poetry and thus Majaz has often been described as Keats of Urdu poetry which is only partly true. These are indeed some similarities between Keats and Majaz. Keats in his famous poem 'Ode to a Nightingale' writes :

Here where men sit and hear each other groan
Where palsy shakes a few and sad last gray hair
Where youth grows pale spectre thin and dies
Where but to think is to be full of sorrow
And laden eyed despair
Where Beauty cannot keep her lustrous eye
... beyond tomorrow

And Majaz wrote :

इस महल की आड़ से निकला है पीला माहताब
जैसे मुल्ला का अमामा जैसे बनिये की किताब
जैसे मुफ़लिस की जवानी जैसा बेवा का शबाब

(The pale moon emerges behind this palace
Like the turban of a mullah like a traders's book

Like a poor man's youth, like a youthful widow's look)

and

मुन्तज़र है एक तूफ़ाने बला मेरे लिये
अब भी जाने कितने दरवाज़े हैं वा मेरे लिये
पर मुसीबत है मेरा अहदे-वफ़ा मेरे लिये
ऐ दिले-ग़म क्या करूँ ऐ वहशते ग़म क्या करूँ

(A battalion of calamities await me though
A thousand doors will still open for me, I know
But my vow of fidelity is my foe
What do I do, O sad heart, my mad heart)

And in the same poem Majaz campares the pale moon to a youthful widow.

Both Majaz and Keats were poets of love and beauty. Besides their failed love affairs, both Keats and Majaz died relatively young. Keats lived only till the age of twenty six years. Both were romantic poets though, the presence of realism in their poetry distinguishes them from other romantic poets. In the poem Ode to a Nightingale, Keats writes,

"Forlorn the very world is like a bell
To toll me back from my sole self
Adieu the fancy cannot cheat as well"

However in Majaz's days Marxism was at its peak. His realism is the realism of life in general and not socio-economic-political realism. And this is a very big difference between the two poets.

Majaz had great respect for and hope from women. Rather than growing cynical about women because of his personal experience, he considers them an equal and a comrade-in-arm in the task of social change.

तेरे माथे का टीका मर्द की किस्मत का तारा है,
अगर तू साज़े-बेदारी उठा लेती तो अच्छा था
स्नानें खींच ली है सरफिरे बाग़ी जवानों ने
तू सामाने-जराहत अब उठा लेती तो अच्छा था

(The mark on your forehead is a star of man's future
You should be showing your awareness right
The young everywhere are rising in revolt
You should also be showing your might)

तेरे माथे पे ये आँचल बहुत ही खूब है लेकिन
तू इस आँचल को इक परचम बना लेती तो अच्छा था

(The veil sits lovely on your forehead though
You should have made it into a banner even so)

Urdu poets and writers have paid glowing tribute to Majaz. According to Firaq Gorakhpuri, the sparks of poetry left behind by Majaz will for ever shine bright. Addressing Majaz as a magnificent Urdu poet, the critic Ehtasham Hussain salutes him and predicts that Majaz's poetry will live for ever. Commenting on Majaz's nature and personality, Majnu Gora Khpuri remarked that he had not met a more modest person than him in all his life. Whereas Ehtesham Hussain put him in the line of great poets and writers like Keats, Shelley, Byron, Codwell, Durgadas Sarvar, Rattan Lal Sarshar, Manto and Akhtar Sheerani who died young, it was left for Josh Malihabadi to pay the most moving tribute. Shaken by Majaz's death, Josh observed that this world of human beasts, this world of petty plots and mean politics, literary cliquism is not worth living for a noble and sensitive person like Majaz and added that he too was packing up and going soon, "Majaz don't lose heart. Josh too is coming and coming soon. Hold on, Majaz !"

September 2021 **Kuldip Salil**

1770 Outram Line
G.T.B. Nagar, Delhi-110009
E-mail: poetkuldipsalil@gmail.com
Mob.: 9810052245

मजाज़ की कविता

हिन्दी, उर्दू व अंग्रेज़ी के जाने-माने वरिष्ठ शायर, कवि और अनुवादक प्रोफ़ेसर कुलदीप सलिल किसी परिचय के मोहताज नहीं हैं। आप हंसराज कॉलेज, दिल्ली विश्वविद्यालय में लगभग 40 वर्षों तक अंग्रेज़ी के एसोसिएट प्रोफ़ेसर के तौर पर अंग्रेज़ी काव्य पढ़ाते रहे। 'काव्य का मर्म' उनके तन-मन में बसा है। आपने मजाज़ लखनवी की चुनिंदा रचनाओं का अंग्रेज़ी में अनुवाद किया है। अनुवाद इतना खूबसूरत हुआ है कि इस सरस और सहज अनुवाद से शायर की रचनाओं के भाव और अर्थ को पाठक सीधे अपने दिल की गहराइयों में हृदयंगम करते हुए साक्षात् महसूस करता है।

मजाज़ के काव्य की उल्लेखनीय विशेषता है उनकी काव्याभिव्यक्ति में रोमानियत और यथार्थ का एक साथ चहलकदमी करना! उनकी कविता दिल से गुज़रती हुई दिमाग तक पहुँचती है और पाठक के अंतर्मन को वैचारिक स्तर पर उद्वेलित करती है, उसे कहीं भीतर ही भीतर सोचने को विवश करती है। मजाज़ की उर्दू कविता का एक खूबसूरत उदाहरण देखें—

इस महल की आड़ से निकला वो पीला माहताब
जैसे मुल्ला का इमामा जैसे बनिये की किताब
जैसे मुफ़लिस की जवानी जैसा बेवा का शबाब
ऐ ग़मे दिल क्या करूँ ऐ वहशते-दिल क्या करूँ।
बढ़के इस इन्दर-सभा का साज़ो-सामां फूँक दूँ

इसका गुलशन फूँक दूँ उसका शबिस्तां फूँक दूँ
तख्ते-सुलतां क्या है कस्रे-सुलतां फूँक दूँ
ऐ ग़मे-दिल क्या करूँ, ऐ वहशते दिल क्या करूँ।

मजाज़ लखनवी की इन चुनी हुई गज़लों, नज़्मों, कत्तों एवं उनके बेहतरीन अनुवाद को पाठकों के समक्ष प्रस्तुत करते हुए हमें बेहद प्रसन्नता हो रही है। उम्मीद है, सुधी पाठकगण इसका दिल से स्वागत करेंगे।

—ओम सपरा

सितम्बर, 2021
दिल्ली

Contents

ग़ज़लें

नज़्में

Ghazals

ग़ज़लें

कुछ तुझको ख़बर है हम क्या-क्या, ऐ शोरिशे-दौरां[1] भूल गये
वो ज़ुल्फ़े-परीशां[2] भूल गये, वो दीदा-ए-गिरियां[3] भूल गये

ऐ शौक़े-नज़ारा[4] क्या कहिये, नज़रों में कोई सूरत ही नहीं
ऐ ज़ौके-तसव्वुर[5] क्या कीजै, हम सूरते-जानां[6] भूल गये

अब गुल से नज़र मिलती ही नहीं, अब दिल की कली खिलती ही नहीं
ऐ फ़स्ले-बहारां[7] रुख़्सत हो, हम लुत्फ़े-बहारां भूल गये

सब का तो मुदावा[8] कर डाला, अपना ही मुदावा कर न सके
सब के तो गरेबां सी डाले, अपना ही गरेबां भूल गये

ये अपनी वफ़ा का आलम है, अब उनकी जफ़ा को क्या कहिये
इक नश्तरे-ज़ह्र-आगीं[9] रखकर नज़दीके-रगे-जां[10] भूल गये।

Kuchh tujhko khabar hai hum kya-kya, e shorishe-dauran bhool gaye
Wo zulfe-parishan bhool gaye, wo dida-e-giriyan bhool gaye

E shauke-nazara kya kahiye, nazaron mein koi surat hi nahi
E zauke-tasavvur kya kije, hum surate-janan bhool gaye

Ab gulse nazar milti hi nahin, ab dil ki kali khilti hi nahin
E fasale-baharan rukhsat ho, hum lutfe-baharan bhool gaye

Sab ka to mudava kar dala, apna hi mudava kar na sake
Sab ke to gareban si dale, apna hi gareban bhool gaye

Ye apni wafa ka aalam hai, ab unki jafa ko kya kahiye
Ek nashtare-zahar-aagin rakhkar nazdike-rage-jaan bhool gaye

---

1. संसार के उपद्रव 2. बिखरे केश 3. रोती आँखें 4. देखने की चाह 5. कल्पना की प्रवृत्ति 6. प्रेयसी की शक्ल 7. वसंत ऋतु 8. उपचार 9. विष में बुझा हुआ नश्तर 10. शहर के निकट

Those tearful eyes, that wayward hair undone
Do you know, O life's struggle what all we have forgotten

Speak not of our love of beauty, not a shape crosses our eyes
O not even our beloved's face within our imagination lies

I don't even get to see her now, never experience true delight
Adieu, O spring season, I no longer share your joyous spright

Except our own, we have taken care of everybody's passion
Except ourselves, we have everybody else a favour done

Our fidelity on the one hand and her faithlessness on the other are to be seen
We put a poisoned pin near our heart and forgot it clean

सारा आलम गोश-बर-आवाज़ है[1]
आज किन हाथों में दिल का साज़ है

हाँ ज़रा जुर्रत दिखा ऐ जज़्बे-दिल
हुस्न को पर्दे पे अपने नाज़ है

हमनशीं दिल की हक़ीक़त क्या कहूँ
सोज़ में डूबा हुआ इक साज़ है

आपकी मख़्मूर आँखों की क़सम
मेरी मय-ख़्वारी अभी तक राज़ है

→

Sara aalam gosh-bar-aawaz hai
Aaj kin hathon mein dil ka saaz hai

Haan zara jurat dikha e jazbe-dil
Husn ko parde pe apne naaz hai

Humnashin dil ki haqikat kya kahoon
Soz mein duba hua ek saaz hai

Aapki makhmoor aankhon ki kasam
Meri may-khwari abhi tak raaz hai

1. पूरा संसार आवाज़ पर कान लगाये है

The whole world is intently listening
Who is it today, holding my heart's string !

Show a little daring, O my heart's passion
So very proud of her veil is the beautiful one

Ask me not the condition of my heart, honey
It's a musical instrument drowned in agony

By your intoxicating eye, I swear
That my drinking is still a secret affair

→

छुप गये वो साज़े-हस्ती[1] छेड़ कर
अब तो बस आवाज़ ही आवाज़ है

हुस्न को नाहक़[2] पशेमा[3] कर दिया
ऐ जूनूं ये भी कोई अंदाज़ है

सारी महफ़िल जिसपे झूम उट्ठी 'मजाज़'
वो तो आवाज़े-शिकस्ते साज़[4] है

Chhup gaye wo saaze-hasti chhed kar
Ab to bas aawaz hi aawaz hai

Husn ko nahak pashema kar diya
E junoon ye bhi koi andaz hai

Sari Mehfil jispe jhoom utthi 'Majaz'
Wo to aawaze-shikaste saaz hai

---

1. जीवन का संगीत 2. बेवजह 3. पश्चाताप 4. टूटा हुआ साज़

She touched my life-string and hid away somewhere
Her voice only, now I hear

Unnecessarily I troubled the beautiful one-
O my passion, it is not done

O hearing which the whole mehfil O Majaz into raptures went
It was the voice of a broken instrument

जुनूने-शौक़[1] अब भी कम नहीं है
मगर वो आज भी बरहम नहीं है

बहुत मुश्किल है दुनिया का संवरना
तिरी ज़ुल्फ़ों का पेचो-ख़म नहीं है

बहुत कुछ और भी है इस जहां में
ये दुनिया महज़ ग़म ही ग़म नहीं है

तकाज़े क्यों करूँ पैहम[2] न साक़ी
किसे यां फ़िक्रे-बेशो-कम[3] नहीं है

→

Junune-shauk ab bhi kam nahin hai
Magar wo aaj bhi barham nahin hai

Bahut mushkil hai duniya ka sanvarna
Tiri zulfon ka pecho-kham nahin hai

Bahut kuchh aur bhi hai is jahan mein
Ye dunia mahaz gam hi gam nahin hai

Takaze kyon karoon paiham na saqi
Kise yaan fikre-besho-kam nahin hai

---

1. इश्क का उन्माद 2. निरंतर 3. अधिक और कम की चिंता

Intensity of my love is not less in any way
But she is not obliging even today

It is not your tangled hair, my dear
It's very difficult to make this world better

It is not all sorrow and suffering only
The world has a lot else in its kitty

Why shouldn't I be demanding constantly
Who is not counting his loss and gain, here O Saqi

→

उधर मशकूक[1] है मेरी सदाक़त[2]
इधर भी बदगुमानी कम नहीं है

मेरी बरबादियों का हमनशीनो
तुम्हें क्या खुद मुझे भी ग़म नहीं है

अभी बज़्मे-तरब[3] से क्या उठूँ मैं
अभी तो आँख भी पुरनम[4] नहीं है

Udhar mashkook hai meri sadakat
Idhar bhi badgumani kam nahin hai

Meri barbadiyon ka humnashino
Tumhein kya khud mujhe bhi gam nahin hai

Abhi bazme-tarab se kya uthun main
Abhi to aankh bhi purnam nahin hai

---

1. संदिग्ध 2. सच्चाई 3. खुशी की महफ़िल से 4. सजल

Neither my perfect sincerity, she knows
Nor any the less my self-respect goes

For my ruin, O friend, in fact
Not only you, I too have no regret

How can I leave this world of gaiety yet
Even my eyes are not exactly wet

परतवे-साग़रे-सहबा[1] क्या था
रात इक हश्र-सा बर्पा[2] क्या था

क्यों जवानी की मुझे याद आई
मैंने इक ख़्वाब सा देखा क्या था

हुस्न की आँख भी नमनाक[3] हुई
इश्क़ को आपने समझा क्या था

इश्क़ ने आँख झुका ली वरना
हुस्न और हुस्न का पर्दा क्या था

क्यों 'मजाज़' आपने साग़र[4] तोड़ा
आज ये शहर में चर्चा क्या था

Partave-sagare-sahba kya tha
Raat ek hashr-sa barpa kya tha

Kyon jawani ki mujhe yaad aayi
Maine ek khwab sa dekha kya tha

Husn ki aankh bhi namnaak huyi
Ishq ko aapne samjha kya tha

Ishq ne aankh jhuka li varna
Husn aur husn ka parda kya tha

Kyon 'Majaz' aapne sagar toda
Aaj ye shahar mein charcha kya tha

---

1. अंगूरी शराब के प्याले का प्रतिबिंब 2. प्रलय सी मची हुई 3. सजल 4. शराब का प्याला

What was it like the doomsday last night, could I know
What did the shadow of the wine-cup show

Why did I remember my youthful days
What is it that this dreamlike experience says

The eye of even the charming one was wet
Did you think my love was so easy to get

The lover lowered his eyes, otherwise
The beauty and its veil was no big deal

The talk of the town was :
Why did you break the chalice, Majaz

आशिक़ी जांफ़ज़ा[1] भी होती है
और सब्र-आज़मा भी होती है

रूह होती है क़ैफ-पर्वर[2] भी
और दर्द-आशना भी होती है

हुस्न को कर न दे ये शर्मिन्दा
इश्क़ से ये ख़ता[3] भी होती है

बन गई रस्म बादाख़्वारी[4] भी
ये नमाज़ अब क़ज़ा[5] भी होती है

जिसको कहते हैं नाला-ए-बरहम[6]
साज़ में वो सदा[7] भी होती है

Aashiki janfaza bhi hoti hai
Aur sabr-aazama bhi hoti hai

Rooh hoti hai kaif-parvar bhi
Aur dard-aashna bhi hoti hai

Husn ko kar na de ye sharminda
Ishq se ye khata bhi hoti hai

Ban gai rasm badakhawari bhi
Ye namaz ab kaza bhi hoti hai

Jisko kahte hain nala-e-barham
Saaz mein vo sada bhi hoti hai

---

1. प्राणवर्धक 2. आनंदोत्पादक 3. ग़लती 4. शराब पीना 5. समय पर न होने वाली नमाज
6. क्रुद्ध आर्त्तनाद 7. आवाज़

Love is a gift of life to you
But it can test your patience too

Heart is a seat of much pleasure
But with pain also it is quite familiar

Love is quite capable of committing folly
And giving blushes to beauty

Drinking has now become a routine like praying
But this prayer can easily be life-consuming

That which is known as a heart-rending cry
In this instrument such sounds also lie.

निगाहे-लुत्फ़[1] *मत उठ, खूगरे-आलाम*[2] *रहने दे*
हमें नाकाम रहना है, हमें नाकाम रहने दे

किसी मासूम पर बेदाद[3] *का इल्ज़ाम क्या मानी*
ये वहशतखेज़ बातें इश्क़े-बद-अंजाम[4] *रहने दे*

अभी रहने दे दिल में शौक़े-शोरीद के[5] *हंगामे*
अभी सर में मोहब्बत का जुनूने-ख़ाम[6] *रहने दे*

अभी रहने दे कुछ दिन लुत्फ़े-नग़मा, मस्ती-ए-सहबा[7]
अभी ये साज़ रहने दे, अभी ये जाम रहने दे

ब-ई-रिंदी[8] *'मजाज़' इक शायरे-मज़दूरो-दहक़ा*[9] *है*
अगर शहरों में वो बदनाम है बदनाम रहने दे

Nigahe-lutf mat uth, khugare-aalam rahne de
Hamein nakam rahna hai, hamein nakam rahne de

Kisi masum par bedad ka ilzaam kya mani
Ye vahshatkhez batein ishqe-bad-anjaam rahne de

Abhi rahne de dil mein shauke-shorida ke hangame
Abhi sar mein mohabbat ka junoone-kham rahne de

Abhi rahne de kuchh din lutfe-nagma, masti-e-sahaba
Abhi ye saaz rahne de, abhi ye jaam rahne de

B-i-rindi 'Majaz' ek shayare-mazduron-dahakan hai
Agar shaharon mein wo badnam hai badnam rahne de

---

1. कृपादृष्टि 2. दु:खों का अभ्यस्त 3. अत्याचार 4. बुरे परिणाम वाले प्रेम 5. परेशानियों की इच्छा के 6. अपक्व उन्माद 7. शराब की मस्ती 8. ऐसा मद्यप होने पर भी 9. मज़दूरों और किसानों का कवि

Favour me not O lovely eye, let me used to sufferings remain
I would rather be a failure than success in love attain

There is no sense in accusing the innocent one of not reciprocating your feelings
Talk not, O my failed love, of such silly things

Let the storm caused by love in the heart remain
Let the passion its full maturity attain

Let me enjoy a few days more this luxury of poetry and liquor
Let you play a little more on this instrument, let me drink a little longer

Majaz is a poet of peasants and workers, he is a drunkard though
And if the townsmen sneer at him, let it be so

जिगर और दिल को बचाना भी है
नज़र आप ही से मिलाना भी है

मोहब्बत का हर भेद पाना भी है
मगर अपना दामन बचाना भी है

जो दिल तेरे ग़म का निशाना भी है
क़तीले-जफ़ाए-ज़माना[1] भी है

ख़िरद की[2] इताअ़त[3] ज़रूरी सही
यही तो जुनूं[4] का ज़माना भी है

→

Jigar aur dil ko bachana bhi hai
Nazar aap hi se milana bhi hai

Mohabbat ka har bhed pana bhi hai
Magar apna daman bachana bhi hai

Jo dil tere gam ka nishana bhi hai
Qatile-jafae-zamana bhi hai

Khirad ki itaat zaruri sahi
Yahi to junu ka zamana bhi hai

---

1. संसार के अत्याचारों का मारा हुआ 2. बुद्धि की 3. आज्ञा-पालन 4. उन्माद

As my eyes must meet your eyes
I have to see that my heart soul also survive

The mysteries of love too I must unravel
And steer clear of it as well

The heart that is for your love mad
Stricken with the cruelties of the world also feels sad

Holding on to your reason is essential though
There is also the time to beyond it go

→

ये दुनिया, ये उक्बा[1] कहां जाइये,
कहीं अहले-दिल का[2] ठिकाना भी है

मुझे आज साहिल पे रोने भी दो
कि तूफ़ान में मुस्कराना भी है

ज़माने से आगे तो बढ़िये 'मजाज़'
ज़माने को आगे बढ़ाना भी है

Ye duniya, ye ukba kahan jaiye
Kahin ahle-dil ka thikana bhi hai

Mujhe aaj sahil pe rone bhi do
Ki tufaan mein muskarana bhi hai

Zamane se aage to badiye 'Majaz'
Zamane ko aage badana bhi hai

---

1. परलोक 2. दिलवालों, आशिक़ों का

Neither in this world nor the world beyond
Is there a place for people who have a heart

As I must smile in the storm
Allow me to cry too on the shore

Go ahead of your times, Majaz,
As somebody has to help the times to advance

दिले-ख़ूं-गश्ता-ए-जफ़ा पे[1] कहीं
अब करम[2] भी गिरां[3] न हो जाये

तेरे बीमार का खुदा हाफ़िज़
नज़्रे-चारागरां[4] न हो जाये

इश्क़ क्या-क्या न आफ़तें ढाए
हुस्न गर मेह्रबां न हो जाए

मय के[5] आगे ग़मों का कोहे-गिरां[6]
एक पल में धुआं न हो जाए

फिर 'मजाज़' इन दिनों ये ख़तरा है
दिल हलाके-बुतां[7] न हो जाए

Dile-khoon-gashta-e-jafa pe kahin
Ab karam bhi giran na ho jaye

Tere bimar ka khuda hafiz
Nazre-charagaran na ho jaye

Ishq kya-kya na aafatein dhaye
Husn gar mehrban na ho jaye

May ke aage gamon ka kohe-giran
Ek pal mein dhuan na ho jaye

Phir 'Majaz' in dinon ye khatra hai
Dil halaake-butan na ho jaye

---

1. उपेक्षा द्वारा घायल मन पर 2. कृपा 3. बोझल, असह्य 4. उपचारकों की भेंट 5. शराब के 6. बहुत बड़ा पहाड़ 7. सुंदरियों द्वारा हताहत

To this heart wounded with callousness it would appear
Even this kindness now may not help at all, I fear

May God save your afflicted one
Or else I fear that he may be by his physicians undone

But for the beauties' generosity
Love would cause the worst calamity

A mountain of sorrows after a good drink
May turn it into smoke and under the earth sink

These days, Majaz a fear doth lurk
Lest the deadly charm of the lovely ladies should work

कमाले-इश्क़[1] है दीवाना हो गया हूँ मैं
ये किसके हाथ से दामन छुड़ा रहा हूँ मैं

तुम्हीं तो हो जिसे कहती है नाखुदा[2] दुनिया
बचा सको तो बचा लो, कि डूबता हूँ मैं

ये मेरे इश्क़ की मजबूरियाँ मआज़-अल्लाह[3]
तुम्हारा राज़ तुम्हीं से छुपा रहा हूँ मैं

Kamale-ishq hai diwana ho gaya hoon main
Ye kiske hath se daman chhuda raha hoon main

Tumhin to ho jise kahati hai nakhuda duniya
Bacha sako to bacha lo, ki doobta hoon main

Ye mere ishq ki majburiyan maaj-allah
Tumhara raaz tumhin se chhupa raha hoon main

---

1. इश्क़ का चमत्कार 2. नाविक 3. ख़ुदा ही पनाह

It is a miracle of love that I am thus infatuated
And I know not from whose clutches I am trying to get myself extricated

You are the one known the world over to be the oarsman
I am drowning, O save me now if you can

Because of my excessive love, God save me, see what I do
It is your secret that I am trying to hide from you

ख़ुद दिल में रहके आँख से पर्दा करे कोई
हाँ लुत्फ़ जब है पा के भी ढूँढ़ा करे कोई

तुमने तो हुक्मे-तर्क-तमन्ना[1] सुना दिया
किस दिल से आह तर्के-तमन्ना करे कोई

दुनिया लरज़ गई दिले-हिर्मां-नसीब[2] की
इस तरह साज़े-ऐश न छेड़ा करे कोई

मुझको ये आरज़ू वो उठाएं निक़ाब ख़ुद
उनको ये इन्तिज़ार तक़ाज़ा करे कोई

या तो किसी को जुर्रते-दीदार[3] ही न हो
या फिर मिरी निगाह से देखा करे कोई

होती है इसमें हुस्न की तौहीन ऐ 'मजाज़'
इतना न अहले-इश्क़ को[4] रुसवा करे कोई

Khud dil mein rahke aankh se parda kare koi
haan lutf jab hai pake bhi dhoondha kare koi

Tumne to hukme-tark-tamanna suna diya
Kis dil se aah tarke-tamanna kare koi

Duniya laraz gai dile-hirmaan-naseeb ki
Is tarah saaze-eish na chheda kare koi

Mujhko ye aarazu wo uthayein nikaab khud
Unko ye intizaar takaza kare koi

Ya to kisi ko jurrate-didar hi na ho
Ya phir miri nigah se dekha kare koi

Hoti hai ismein husn ki tauhin e 'Majaz'
Itna na ahale-ishq ko ruswa kare koi

---

1. इश्क़ तज देने का हुक्म 2. निराश मन की 3. दर्शनों का साहस 4. प्रेमीजनों को

Somebody should live in the heart and still hide from the eyes
It is in continuing the search even after getting the object that beauty lies

You have so easily issued a diktat against loving
O how can one have the heart to do such a thing

The very foundation of my dejected heart is shaken
Nobody should play like this on his instrument of elation

I wish she lifts the veil on her own behest
But she is waiting for me to make a request

Either one should not make bold to see that sight
Or one should see it with my eyes

O Majaz, it is tantamount to an insult to beauty
Nobody should treat the lover so severely

नहीं ये फ़िक्र कोई रहबरे-कामिल[1] नहीं मिलता
कोई दुनिया में मानूसे-मिज़ाजे-दिल[2] नहीं मिलता

कभी साहिल पे रहकर शौक़ तूफ़ानों से टकराएं
कभी तूफ़ां में रहकर फ़िक्र है साहिल नहीं मिलता

ये आना कोई आना है कि बस रस्मन चले आए
ये मिलना ख़ाक मिलना है कि दिल से दिल नहीं मिलता

वहाँ कितनों को तख़्तो-ताज का अरमां है क्या कहिए
जहाँ साइल[3] को अक्सर कासा-ए-साइल[4] नहीं मिलता

ये क़त्ले-आम और बे-इज़्न क़त्ले-आम[5] क्या कहिए
ये बिस्मिल[6] कैसे बिस्मिल हैं जिन्हें क़ातिल नहीं मिलता

Nahin ye fikra koi rahbare-kamil nahin milta
Koi duniya mein manuse-mizaje-dil nahin milta

Kabhi sahil pe rahkar shauk tufanon se takrayein
Kabhi tufan mein rahkar fikra hai sahil nahin milta

Ye aana koi aana hai ki bas rasman chale aaye
Ye milna khaak milna hai ki dil se dil nahin milta

Wahan kitnon ko takhto-taaj ka armaan hai kya kahiye
Jahan saail ko aksar kasa-e-saail nahin milta

Ye qatle-aam aur be-izan qatle-aam kya kahiye
Ye bismil kaise bismil hain jinhein qatil nahin milta

---

1. सिद्ध पथ-प्रदर्शक 2. स्वभाव से परिचित (मित्र) 3. भिखारी 4. भिक्षा-पात्र 5. निर्देश बिना सर्व-संहार 6. आहत

The problem is not that we don't have a proper guide
It is that we don't have a bosom friend by our side

Sometimes when we are on the shore, we wish we were at the storm's door
And when we are in the midst of it, we want to be on the shore

This formal visit is no visit at all
What kind of meeting is this if there is no meeting of hearts

O how very many people yearn for the throne and crown here
While for the beggar we cannot even a begging bowl spare

This massacre, this mindless massacre is strange indeed
The murdered ones don't know who has done the deed

दामने-दिल पे[1] नहीं बारिशे-इल्हाम[2] अभी
इश्क़ नापुख़्ता[3] अभी, जज़्बे दरूं[4] ख़ाम[5] अभी

खुद झिझकता हूँ कि दावा-ए-जुनूं[6] क्या कीजै
कुछ गवारा भी है ये क़ैदे-दरो-वाम[7] अभी

ये जवानी तो अभी माइले-पैकार[8] नहीं
ये जवानी तो है रुसवाए-मय-ओ-जाम[9] अभी

Daamane-dil pe nahin barishe-ilhaam abhi
Ishq napukhta abhi, jazbe daroon kham abhi

Khud jhijhakta hoon ki dava-e-junoon kya kije
Khuchh gavara bhi hai ye kaide-daro-vaam abhi

Ye jawani to abhi maaile-paikar nahin
Ye jawani to hai ruswaaye-may-o-jaam abhi

---

1. दिल रूपी दामन पर 2. दैवी प्रेरणा की वर्षा 3. अपरिपक्व 4. भीतरी भावना 5. अपक्व 6. उन्माद का दावा 7. दरवाज़ों और छतों (घर) की क़ैद 8. संघर्ष की ओर प्रवृत्त 9. शराब के कारण बदनाम

My heart as yet is not visited by divine inspiration
Love is not deep enough nor as yet an intense passion

I cannot claim that my love as yet passionately soars
I doubt if I am quite ready to be confined indoors

My youth as yet is to drinking lost
It is not ready yet for the struggle long and vast

हुस्न की बज़्मे-ख़ास में जाकर इससे ज़ियादा क्या होगा
कोई नया पैमां[1] बाँधेंगे, कोई नया वादा होगा

चारागरी[2] सर आँखों पर इस चारागारी से क्या होगा
दर्द कि अपनी आप दवा है, तुमसे अच्छा क्या होगा

वाइज़े-सादालौह से[3] कह दो छोड़ उक़्बा की[4] बातें
इस दुनिया में क्या रखा है, उस दुनिया में क्या होगा

तुम भी 'मजाज़' इन्सान हो आख़िर लाख छुपाओ इश्क़ अपना
ये भेद मगर खुल जाएगा, ये राज़ मगर अफ़शा[5] होगा

Husn ki bazme-khaas mein jakar isse ziyada kya hoga
Koi naya paiman bandhenge, koi naya wada hoga

Charagari sar aankhon par is charagari se kya hoga
Dard ki apni aap dava hai, tumse achchha kya hoga

Waije-sadalauh se kah do chhod ukba ki batein
Is duniya mein kya rakha hai, us duniya mein kya hoga

Tum bhi 'Majaz' insaan ho aakhir lakh chhupao ishq apna
Ye bhed magar khul jayega, ye raaz magar afasha hoga

---

1. प्रतिज्ञा 2. उपचार 3. सरल स्वभाव धर्मोपदेशक से 4. परलोक की 5. प्रकट

We will get a new promise, a contract new
In beauty's august assembly what more can we hope to do

Your treatment, I welcome but how can your treatment cure
Pain is its own cure what can you do more

Tell the simple-minded preacher not to pin hope, on the other world, sir
What is this world worth, what will be there in the other world either !

Majaz, you too are a man after all, however much you hide
This secret will be out, it cannot be kept inside

साज़गार[1] है हमदम[2] इन दिनों जहाँ अपना
इश्क़ शादमां[3] अपना, शौक़[4] कामरां[5] अपना

आह बेअसर किसकी, नाला[6] नारसा[7] किसका
काम वारहा आया जज़्बा-ए-निहां[8] अपना

कब किया था इस दिल पर हुस्न ने करम[9] इतना
मेहरबान इस दर्जा, कब था आस्मां अपना

इश्क़ और रुसवाई कौन सी नई शै है
इश्क़ तो अज़ल से[10] था रुसवाए-जहां अपना

तुम 'मजाज़' दीवाने मसलहत से बेगाने[11]
वरना हम बना लेते तुमको राजदां[12] अपना

Saazgar hai hamdam in dinon jahan apna
Ishq shadmaan apna, Shauk kaamraan apna

Aah beasar kiski, nala narsa kiska
Kaam Warha aaya jazba-e-nihan apna

Kab kiya tha is dil par husn ne karam itna
Mehrban is darja, kab tha aasman apna

Ishq aur ruswai kaun si nai shai hai
Ishq to azal se tha ruswaye-jahan apna

Tum 'Majaz' diwane masalhat se begane
Warna hum bana lete tumko razdan apna

---

1. अनुकूल 2. साथी 3. इश्क़ 4. आह्लादित 5. सफल 6. आर्त्तनाद 7. न पहुँचने वाला 8. निहित भावना 9. कृपा 10. आदिकाल से 11. हित से अपरिचित 12. भेदी

My love is successful these days, my passion is well rewarded
I find that I was never by this world better regarded

Who says my sighs are ineffective, my cries are unheard
So often has my hidden passion my purpose so well served

My beloved to me was never so kind
Heavens towards me are really well-inclined

There is nothing new in our love being disgraced
Love has for ever and ever this infamy faced

You are an infatuated one O Majaz who not even his self interest knows
Otherwise we would have made you our confidante close

रहे-शौक़ से[1] अब हटा चाहता हूँ
कशिश[2] हुस्न की देखना चाहता हूँ

कोई दिल-सा दर्द-आशना चाहता हूँ
रहे-इश्क़ में रहनुमा[3] चाहता हूँ

तुझी से तुझे छीनना चाहता हूँ
ये क्या चाहता हूँ, ये क्या चाहता हूँ

ख़ताओं पे[4] जो मुझको माइल[5] करे फिर
सज़ा और ऐसी सज़ा चाहता हूँ

Rahe-shauk se ab hata chahta hoon
Kashish husn ki dekhna chahta hoon

Koi dil-sa dard-aashna chahta hoon
Rahe-ishq mein rahnuma chahta hoon

Tujhi se tujhe chhinna chahta hoon
Ye kya chahta hoon, ye kya chahta hoon

Khataon pe jo mujhko maail kare phir
Sazaa aur aesi sazaa chahta hoon

1. इश्क़ के मार्ग 2. आकर्षण 3. पथप्रदर्शक 4. ग़लतियों पर 5. प्रवृत्त

I think I should stop loving now
How much attraction beauty has in it, let it show,

I need somebody who understands my suffering like
my heart
And play in this journey of love a guide's part

From yourself, I want to snatch you
See what it is that I wish to do

That which induces me to make mistakes again
I want such punishment, such punishment I want

ये जहां बारगहे-रत्ले-गिरां[1] है साक़ी
इक जहन्नुम मिरे सीने में तपां है[2] साक़ी

जिसने बर्बाद किया माइले-.फ़रियाद[3] किया
वो मोहब्बत अभी इस दिल में जवां है साक़ी

माहो-अंजुम[4] मिरे अश्कों से गुहरताब[5] हुए
कहकशां[6] नूर की इक जूए-रवां[7] है साक़ी

हुस्न ही हुस्न है जिस सिम्त[8] भी उठती है नज़र
कितना पुरकै.फ़ ये[9] मंज़र[10] ये समां है[11] साक़ी

मेरे हर ल.फ़्ज़ में बेताब मिरा सोज़े-दरूं[12]
मेरी हर साँस मोहब्बत का धुआं है साक़ी

Ye jahan baargahe-ratle-giran hai saki
Ek jahnnum mire sine mein tapa hai saki

Jisne barbad kiya maaile-fariyad kiya
Vo mohabbat abhi is dil mein javan hai saki

Maho-anjum mire ashkon se guhartab hue
Kahkashan noor ki ek juye-rawan hai saki

Husn hi husn hai jis simt bhi uthti hai nazar
Kitna purkaif ye manzar ye samaan hai saki

Mere har lafz mein betab mira soze-daroon
Meri har sans mohabbat ka dhuan hai saki

---

1. बहुमूल्य शराब के प्याले की राजसभा (मधुशाला) 2. जल रहा है 3. फ़रियाद करने पर विवश 4. चाँद, सितारे 5. आँसुओं से मोतियों जैसे चमकदार 6. आकाश-गंगा 7. प्रकाश की बहती नदी 8. ओर 9. आनन्ददायक 10. दृश्य 11. समय 12. भीतरी जलन

A strange wine is flowing in the tavern of world,
O Saqi
And in my heart burns an inferno O Saqi

The love that ruined and compelled me to sue for
mercy
The same love still warms my heart, O Saqi

My tears blessed the sun and moon with pearl-like
shine and beauty
And the galaxy there is a stream of light O Saqi

A sheet of beauty spreads where ever we see
How lovely look the scene and atmosphere O Saqi

Through every breath I take, comes out the pain in
my restless heart
With every breath comes out the wind of my failed
love O Saqi

इस इक हिजाब पे[1] सौ बेहिजाबियां सदक़े
जहाँ से चाहता हूँ तुमको देखता हूँ मैं

बताने वाले वहीं पर बताते हैं मंज़िल
हज़ार बार जहाँ से गुज़र चुका हूँ मैं

कभी ये ज़ो'म[2] कि तू मुझसे छुप नहीं सकता
कभी ये वहम कि खुद भी छुपा हुआ हूँ मैं

मुझे सुने न कोई मस्ते-बादा-ए-इश्रत[3]
'मजाज़' टूटे हुए दिल की इक सदा[4] हूँ मैं

Is ek hijab pe sau behijabiyan sadake
Jahan se chahta hoon tumko dekhta hoon main

Batane wale vahin par batate hain manzil
Hazar baar jahan se guzar chuka hoon main

Kabhi ye zo'm ki tu mujhse chhup nahi sakta
Kabhi ye vaham ki khud bhi chhupa hua hoon main

Mujhe sune na koi maste-bada-e-ishrat
'Majaz' tute hue dil ki ek sada hoon main

---

1. पर्दे पर 2. घमंड 3. सुख-रूपी शराब द्वारा मस्त 4. आवाज़

For this one veil, without a hundred unveiled faces
I can do
For, wherever I like I can see you

The knowledgeable people say
That I have passed the destination a thousand times
on the way

Sometime I feel confident that you just cannot hide
yourself from me
And sometime I doubt if even my own self I can see

The sound of a broken heart, O Majaz echoes through
my poetry
It is not meant for people who are happy and lucky

हुस्न फिर फ़ित्नागर[1] है क्या कहिए
दिल की जानिब नज़र है क्या कहिए

फिर वही रहगुज़र है, क्या कहिए
ज़िंदगी राह पर है, क्या कहिए

आह तो बे-असर थी बरसों से
नग़मा भी बे-असर है, क्या कहिए

हुस्न है अब न हुस्न के जलवे
अब नज़र ही नज़र है, क्या कहिए

आज भी है 'मजाज़' ख़ाक-नशीं[2]
और नज़र अर्श पर[3] है, क्या कहिए

Husn phir fitnagar hai kya kahiye
Dil ki janib nazar hai kya kahiye

Phir wahi rahgujar hai, kya kahiye
Zindgi raah par hai, kya kahiye

Aah to be-asar thi barson se
Nagma bhi be-asar hai, kya kahiye

Husn hai ab na husn ke jalve
Ab nazar hi nazar hai, kya kahiye

Aaj bhi hai 'Majaz' khak-nashin
Aur nazar arsh par hai, kya kahiye

---

1. उपद्रवशील, 2. धरती पर रहने वाला 3. आकाश पर

Beauty is once again on the riotous path, what do you say
Its eyes are turned towards the heart, what do you say

It is the same pathway, what do you say
Life is no longer going astray, what do you say

Our sighs had no effect earlier too
Now our song is also ineffective, what do we do

Beauty is a thing of the past, a thing of the past its charm too
Only the thirsty eyes remain, what do we do

Majaz's feet are on the earth even today
But his eyes are fixed on the sky, what do you say

अक़्ल की सतह से[1] कुछ और उभर जाना था
इश्क़ को मंज़िले-पस्ती से[2] गुज़र जाना था

हुस्न का ग़म भी हसीं, फ़िक्र हसीं, दर्द हसीं
उनको हर रंग में हर तौर संवर जाना था

ये तो क्या कहिए चला था मैं कहाँ से हमदम[3]
मुझको ये भी न था मालूम किधर जाना था

हुस्न, और इश्क़ को दे ता'ना-ए-बेदाद[4] 'मजाज़'
तुमको तो सिर्फ़ इसी बात पे मर जाना था

Akl ki satah se kuchh aur ubhar jana tha
Ishq ko ṃanzile-pasti se guzar jana tha

Husn ka gam bhi hansin, fikra hansi, dard hansi
Unko har rang mein har taur sanvar jana tha

Ye to kya kahiye chala tha main kahan se hamdam
Mujhko ye bhi na tha maloom kidhar jana tha

Husn, aur ishq ko de ta'na-e-bedad 'Majaz'
Tumko to sirf isi baat pe mar jana tha

---

1. स्तर से 2. पतन की मंज़िल से 3. साथी 4. अत्याचार का ताना

I should have risen above the level of ordinary common sense
And not succumbed to a feeling of depression in love

Thinking, suffering, pain – everything relating to beauty is charming
I should have been embellished by it in whatever form it came

What shall I say from where my journey started
I did not know for where I was headed either

You should have known the infidelity of love and beauty
And that should have been the end of your adventurous journey

इज़्मे ख़िराम[1] लेते हुए आस्मां से हम
हटकर चले हैं रहगुज़रे-कारवां से[2] हम

क्योंकर हुआ है .फ़ाश[3] ज़माने पे क्या कहें
वो राज़े-दिल जो कह न सके राज़दां से[4] हम

हमदम यही है रहगुज़रे-यारे-खुश-ख़िराम[5]
गुज़रे हैं लाख बार इसी कहकशां से[6] हम

क्या-क्या हुआ है हमसे जुनूं में न पूछिए
उलझे कभी ज़मीं से कभी आस्मां से हम

ठुकरा दिए हैं अक्लो-ख़िरद के[7] सनमकदे[8]
घबरा चुके थे कश्मकशे-इम्तिहां से हम

बख्शी हैं हमको इश्क़ ने वो जुर्रतें मजाज़
डरते नहीं सियासते-अहले-जहां से[9] हम

Izme khiram lete hue aasman se ham
Hatkar chale hain rahgujare-karwan se ham

Kyonkar hua hai faash zamane pe kya kahein
Wo raze-dil jo kah na sake raajdan se ham

Hamdam yahi hai rahgujare-yare-khush-khiram
Gujare hain lakh baar isi kahkashan se ham

Kya-Kya hua hai hamse junoon mein na puchhiye
Uljhe kabhi zamin se kabhi aasman se ham

Thukra diye hain aklo-khirad ke sanamkade
Ghabra chuke the kashmkashe-imtihan se ham

Bakhshi hain hamko ishq ne vo jurratein Majaz
Darte nahin siyasate-ahle-jahan se ham

---

1. धीमी चाल से चलने का आदेश 2. कारवान के रास्ते से 3. प्रकट 4. भेदी से 5. सुंदर चाल से चलने वाले यार (प्रेयसी) का मार्ग 6. आकाशगंगा से 7. बुद्धि और होश के 8. मंदिर 9. संसार वालों की राजनीति से

Instructed by heaven to go slow
On a road, away from the highway, we decided to go

It became public knowledge, I know not how,
The secret, which even my confidant did not know

This is the road, O friend, which my beloved had taken with her lovely gait
This is the milky way I travelled a million times at any rate

What all we have gone through while in love, O ask not
Sometimes, we had a tiff with the earth, sometimes, with heaven fought

Much harried by being put to test repeatedly
We have thrown common sense and discretion to winds already

On the strength of our love, O Majaz, we do and dare,
About the politicking of the petty world, we do not care

Nazms
नज़्में

आवारा

शहर की रात और मैं नाशादो-नाकारा[1] फिरूँ
जगमगाती जागती सड़कों पे आवारा फिरूँ
ग़ैर की बस्ती है, कब तक दर-ब-दर मारा फिरूँ
ऐ गमे-दिल क्या करूँ, ऐ वहशते-दिल क्या करूँ!

झिलमिलाते कुमकुमों की[2] राह में ज़ंजीर सी
रात के हाथों में दिल की मोहनी तस्वीर सी
मेरे सीने पर मगर दहकी हुई शमशीर[3] सी
ऐ ग़मे-दिल क्या करूँ, ऐ वहशते-दिल क्या करूँ!

ये रुपहली[4] छाँव, ये आकाश पर तारों का जाल
जैसे सूफ़ी का तसव्वुर[5], जैसे आशिक़ का ख़याल
आह लेकिन कौन जाने, कौन समझे जी का हाल
ऐ ग़मे-दिल क्या करूँ, ऐ वहशते-दिल क्या करूँ!

→

Shahar ki raat aur main nashado-nakara phirun
Jagmagati jaagati sadakon pe aawara phirun
Gair ki basti hai, kab tak dar-b-dar mara phirun
E game-dil kya karun, E vahshate-dil kya karun!

Jhilmilate kumkumon ki raah mein zanjir si
Raat ke hathon mein dil ki mohni tasvir si
Mere sine par magar dahaki huyi shamshir si
E game-dil kya karun, E vahshate-dil kya karun!

Ye rupahali chhanv, ye aakash par taron ka jaal
Jaise sufi ka tasavvur, jaise aashik ka khayal
Aah lekin kaun jane, kaun samajhe ji ka haal
E game-dil kya karun, E vahshate-dil kya karun!

---

1. उदास और बेकार 2. बिजली की बत्तियों की 3. तलवार 4. चाँदी-रंग 5. अनुध्यान

The Vagabond

This nightfall in the city, and I wander aimless and sad
On the awake and glittering road, my aimless wandering, O

How long in the alien city from door to door I got
What do I do, O sad heart, my mad heart !

There is a chain of glittering lights all the way
The night holds in its hand the lovely image of the morning ahead

But on my heart, I have a sword burning red
What do I do, O sad heart, my mad heart !

This silvery shade, this net of stars on the sky
Like the philosopher's imagination, like the lovers flight
But ah, who will know, who will feel my heart's plight!
What do I do, O sad heart, my mad heart !

→

फिर वो टूटा इक सितारा, फिर वो छूटी फुलझड़ी
जाने किसकी गोद में आई ये मोती की लड़ी
हूक़-सी सीने में उठी, चोट-सी दिल पर पड़ी
ऐ ग़मे-दिल क्या करूँ, ऐ वहशते-दिल क्या करूँ!

रात हँस-हँस के ये कहती है कि मैखाने[1] में चल
फिर किसी शाहनाज़े-लाल-रूख के[2] काशाने में[3] चल
ये नहीं मुमकिन तो फिर ऐ दोस्त वीराने में चल
ऐ ग़मे-दिल क्या करूँ, ऐ वहशते-दिल क्या करूँ!

हर तरफ़ बिखरी हुई रंगीनियाँ, रा'नाइयाँ[4]
हर क़दम पर इश्रते[5] लेती हुई अँगड़ाइयाँ
बढ़ रही हैं गोद फैलाए हुए रुसवाइयाँ
ऐ ग़मे-दिल क्या करूँ, ऐ वहशते-दिल क्या करूँ!

→

Phir wo tuta ek sitara, phir wo chhuti phuljhari
Jane kiski god mein aai ye moti ki ladi
hook-si sine mein uthi, chot-si dil par padi
E game-dil kya karun, E vahshate-dil kya karun!

Raat hans-hans ke ye kahti hai ki maikhane mein chal
Phir kisi shaahnaze-lal-rookh ke kashane mein chal
Ye nahin mumkin to phir E dost virane mein chal
E game-dil kya karun, E vahshate-dil kya karun!

Har taraf bikhari hui ranginiyan, ra'naiyan
Har kadam par ishrate leti hui angdaiyan
Badh rahi hain god failaye huye ruswaiyan
E game-dil kya karun, E vahshate-dil kya karun!

---

1. मधुशाला 2. लाल के फूल-ऐसे मुखड़े वाली के 3. मकान में 4. खूबसूरती 5. सुख-भोग

A star falls again, again there is a dancing light,
God knows in whose lap this garland of pearls will go
But there is a cry welling up, and on my heart I feel a blow
What do I do, O sad heart, my mad heart !

I am egged on by the smiling night to head for the tavern,
To the house of a blooming beauty bend,
And if this is not possible, proceed to the wilderness, O friend
What do I do, O sad heart, my mad heart !

On every side I see colour and gaiety,
On every side expanded beauty,
But I'm proceeding towards infamy only-
What do I do, O sad heart, my mad heart !

→

रास्ते में रुक के दम ले लूँ, मिरी आदत नहीं
लौटकर वापस चला जाऊँ, मिरी फ़ितरत[1] नहीं
और कोई हमनवा[2] मिल जाए, ये किस्मत नहीं
ऐ ग़मे-दिल क्या करूँ, ऐ वहशते-दिल क्या करूँ!

मुन्तज़िर है एक तूफ़ाने-वला[3] मेरे लिए
अब भी जाने कितने दरवाज़े हैं वा मेरे लिए
पर मुसीबत है मिरा अहदे-वफ़ा[4] मेरे लिए
ऐ ग़मे-दिल क्या करूँ, ऐ वशहते-दिल क्या करूँ!

जी में आता है कि अब अहदे-वफ़ा भी तोड़ दूँ
उनको पा सकता हूँ मैं, ये आसरा भी तोड़ दूँ
हाँ मुनासिब है, ये ज़ंजीरे-हवा[5] भी तोड़ दूँ
ऐ ग़मे-दिल क्या करूँ, ऐ वहशते-दिल क्या करूँ!

→

Raste mein ruk ke dam le loon, miri aadat nahin
Lautkar wapas chala jaaun, miri fitrat nahin
Aur koi hamnava mil jaye, ye kismat nahin
E game-dil kya karun, E vahshate-dil kya karun!

Muntzir hai ek tufane-vala mere liye
Ab bhi jane kitne darwaze hain va mere liye
Par musibat hai mira ahade-wafa mere liye
E game-dil kya karun, E vahshate-dil kya karun!

Ji mein aata hai ki ab ahade-wafa bhi tod doon
Unko pa sakta hoon main, ye aasara bhi tod doon
Han munasib hai, ye zanjire-hawa bhi tod doon
E game-dil kya karun, E vahshate-dil kya karun!

---

1. स्वभाव या प्रकृति 2. साथी 3. विपत्तियों का तूफ़ान 4. प्रेम निभाने की प्रतिज्ञा 5. वायु की ज़ंजीर

To stop by and rest is not my habit
It's alien to my nature to turn back and go
But I'm not lucky enough to meet some friend, I know-
What do I do, O sad heart, my mad heart !

A battalion of calamities awaits me though
A thousand doors will still open for me, I know
But my vow of fidelity, is my foe
What do I do, O sad heart, my mad heart !

I feel like breaking this vow of fidelity now
I shall give up all hope of attaining her
To break this useless bond is perhaps better
What do I do, O sad heart, my mad heart !

→

इक महल की आड़ से निकला वो पीला माहताब[1]
जैसे मुल्ला का अमामा[2], जैसे बनिए की किताब
जैसे मुफ़लिस[3] की जवानी, जैसे बेवा का शबाब[4]
ऐ ग़मे-दिल क्या करूँ, ऐ वहशते-दिल क्या करूँ!

दिल में इक शो'ला भड़क उट्ठा है, आख़िर क्या करूँ
मेरा पैमाना छलक उट्ठा है, आखिर क्या करूँ
ज़ख़्म सीने में महक उट्ठा है, आखिर क्या करूँ
ऐ ग़मे-दिल क्या करूँ, ऐ वहशते-दिल क्या करूँ!

जी में आता है ये मुर्दा चाँद-तारे नोच लूँ
इस किनारे नोच लूँ और उस किनारे नोच लूँ
एक-दो का ज़िक्र क्या, सारे के सारे नोच लूँ
ऐ ग़मे-दिल क्या करूँ, ऐ वहशते-दिल क्या करूँ!

→

Ik mahal ki aad se nikala wo pila mahtab
Jaise mulla ka amama, jaise baniye ki kitab
Jaise muflis ki jawani, jaise beva ka shabab
E game-dil kya karun, E vahshate-dil kya karun!

Dil mein ek shola bhadak uttha hai, aakhir kya karun
Mera paimana chhalak uttha hai, aakhir kya karun
Zakhm sine mein mahak uttha hai, aakhir kya karun
E game-dil kya karun, E vahshate-dil kya karun!

Ji mein aata hai ye murda chand-taare noch loon
Is kinare noch loon aur us kinare noch loon
Ek-do ka zikra kya, sare ke sare noch loon
E game-dil kya karun, E vahshate-dil kya karun!

---

1. चाँद 2. पगड़ी 3. निर्धन 4. यौवन

The pale moon emerges from behind the palace
Like the turban of a mullah, like a trader's book
Like a poor man's youth, like a youthful widow's withered look-
What do I do, O sad heart, my mad heart !

There is a fire in my heart, what should I do
My patience breaks apart, what shall I do
More I dress the wound, greater is the smart, what should I do
What do I do, O sad heart, my mad heart !

I feel like plucking out the moon and the stars dead
Plucking out from this side, plucking out from that
Not one or two, but all of them, plucking out flat
What do I do, O sad heart, my mad heart !

→

मुफ़लिसी और ये मज़ाहिर[1] हैं नज़र के सामने
सैकड़ों सुलताने-जाबिर[2] हैं नज़र के सामने
सैकड़ों चंगेज़ो-नादिर हैं नज़र के सामने
ऐ ग़मे-दिल क्या करूँ, वे वहशते-दिल क्या करूँ!

लेके इक चंगेज़ के हाथों से ख़ंजर तोड़ दूँ
ताज पर उसके दमकता है जो पत्थर तोड़ दूँ
कोई तोड़े या न तोड़े मैं ही बढ़कर तोड़ दूँ
ऐ ग़मे-दिल क्या करूँ, वे वहशते-दिल क्या करूँ!

बढ़ के इस इन्दर-सभा का साज़ो-सामां फूँक दूँ
इसका गुलशन फूँक दूँ, उसका शबिस्ता[3] फूँक दूँ
तख़्ते-सुल्तां[4] क्या, मैं सारा क़स्रे-सुल्तां[5] फूँक दूँ
ऐ ग़मे-दिल क्या करूँ, ऐ वहशते-दिल क्या करूँ!

Muflisi aur ye mazahir hain nazar ke samne
Saikadon sultane-jaabir hain nazar ke samne
Saikadon changezo-nadir hain nazar ke samne
E game-dil kya karun, E vahshate-dil kya karun!

Leke ik changez ke hathon se khanjar tod doon
Taj par uske damakata hai jo patthar tod doon
Koi tode ya na tode main hi badkar tod doon
E game-dil kya karun, E vahshate-dil kya karun!

Badke is Inder-sabha ka sazo-saman phoonk doon
Iska gulshan phoonk doon, uska shabista phoonk doon
Takhte-sultan kya, main sara kasre-sultan phoonk doon
E game-dil kya karun, E vahshate-dil kya karun!

---

1. नज़ारे 2. अत्याचारी बादशाह 3. शयनागार 4. बादशाह का सिंहासन 5. शाही महल

A state of penury here, and these sights before my eyes
A Changez Khan and a Nadir Shah strutting proudly
A thousand kings and their cruelty before me I see
What do I do, O sad heart, my mad heart !

I shall snatch the sword from Changez's hand and break it apart
The glittering stone in his crown I must hit
Some body else may or may not, but I should break it
What do I do, O sad heart, my mad heart !

I should rise and burn all the paraphernalia in Lord Indra's court
Burn this garden and set that bedroom ablaze
Why only the courtroom, the entire palace to the ground raze
What do I do, O sad heart, my mad heart !

नौजवान ख़ातून से

हिजाबे-फ़ित्ना-परवर[1] अब उठा लेती तो अच्छा था
खुद अपने हुस्न को पर्दा बना लेती तो अच्छा था

तिरी नीची नज़र खुद तेरी इस्मत की मुहाफ़िज़ है
तू इस नश्तर की तेज़ी आज़मा लेती तो अच्छा था

तिरी चीने-जबीं[2] खुद इक सज़ा कानूने-फ़ितरत में
इसी शमशीर से कारे-सज़ा[3] लेती तो अच्छा था

ये तेरा ज़र्द रुख[4], ये खुश्क लब, ये वहम, ये वहशत
तू अपने सर से ये बादल हटा लेती तो अच्छा था

दिले-मजरूह को[5] मजरूहतर करने से क्या हासिल
तू आँसू पोंछकर अब मुस्करा लेती तो अच्छा था

→

Hijabe-fitna-parvar ab utha leti to achchha tha
Khud apne husn ko parda bana leti to achchha tha

Tiri nichi nazar khud teri ismat ki muhafiz hai
Tu is nashtar ki tezi aazama leti to achchha tha

Tiri chine-jabin khud ik sazaa kanune-fitrat mein
Isi shamshir se kare-sazaa leti to achchha tha

Ye tera zard rukh, ye khushk lab, ye vaham, ye vahshat
Tu apne sar se ye badal hata leti to achchha tha

Dile-majrooh ko majroohtar karne se kya hasil
Tu aansu ponchhkar ab muskara leti to achchha tha

---

1. उपद्रवकर्ता पर्दा 2. माथे का बल 3. दंड देने का कार्य 4. पीला मुखड़ा 5. घायल हृदय को

To a young Lady

Better, you had removed the malevolent veil now,
Better, you had put on a veil of your own beauty,

Your shyness is itself a guarantee of your dignity
You had better tested this weapon's efficacy

The crease on your forehead is a natural chastisement
You should have used this sword to award punishment, instead.

Your pale face, your dry lips, your fears irrational
Better, you had removed this cloud-cover from over your head,

What use, further hurting the bruised heart,
You had better wipe your tears and smile prithee,

→

अगर ख़लवत में[1] तूने सर उठाया भी तो क्या हासिल
भरी महफ़िल में आकर सर झुका लेती तो अच्छा था

तिरे माथे का टीका मर्द की क़िस्मत का तारा है
अगर तू साज़े-बेदारी[2] उठा लेती तो अच्छा था

सिनाने[3] खैंच ली हैं सर-फिरे बाग़ी जवानों ने
तू सामाने-जराहत[4] अब उठा लेती तो अच्छा था

तिरे माथे पे ये आँचल बहुत ही खूब है लेकिन
तू इस आंचल से इक परचम[5] बना लेती तो अच्छा था

(1937)

Agar khalwat mein tune sar uthaya bhi to kya hasil
Bhari mahfil mein aakar sar jhuka leti to achchha tha

Tire mathe ka tika mard ki kismat ka tara hai
Agar tu saaze-bedari utha leti to achchha tha

Sinane khainch li hain sar-phire bagi jawanon ne
Tu samane-jarahat ab utha leti to achchha tha

Tire mathe pe ye aanchal bahut hi khoob hai lekin
Tu is aanchal se ik parcham bana leti to achchha tha

(1937)

---

1. एकांत में 2. जागरण का साज़ 3. भाले 4. शल्य-चिकित्सा-सम्बन्धी सामग्री 5. पताका

In private, if you raise your head, it is no use,
Even if you had to bow your head, you should bow it
before a full assembly.

The mark on your forehead is a star of man's future
You should be showing your awareness right

The young everywhere are rising in revolt
You should also be showing your might.

The veil sits lovely on your forehead though
You should have made it into a banner even so

साक़ी

मिरी मस्ती में अब होश ही का तौर[1] है साक़ी
तिरे साग़र में ये सहबा[2] नहीं कुछ और है साक़ी

भड़कती जा रही है दम-ब-दम इक आग-सी दिल में
ये कैसे जाम हैं साक़ी, ये कैसा दौर है साक़ी

वो शै दे जिससे नींद आ जाए अक़्ले-फ़ित्ना-परवर को[3]
कि दिल आजुर्दहे-तमईज़े-लुत्फ़ो-जौर[4] है साक़ी

जवानी और यूँ घिर जाए तूफ़ाने-हवादिस में[5]
ख़ुदा रक्खे अभी तो बेख़ुदी का दौर है साक़ी

→

Miri masti mein ab hosh hi ka taur hai saqi
Tire saagar mein ye sahba nahin kuchh aur hai saqi

Bhadakati ja rahi hai dam-b-dam ik aag-si dil mein
Ye kaise jaam hain saqi, ye kaisa daur hai saqi

Wo shai de jisse nind aa jaye akle-fitna-parvar ko
Ki dil aajurdahe-tamaize-lutfo-jaur hai saqi

Jawani aur yun ghir jaye tufane-havadis mein
Khuda rakkhe abhi to bekhudi ka daur hai saqi

---

1. रंग-ढंग 2. अंगूरी शराब 3. उपद्रव खड़े करने वाली बुद्धि 4. अनुकम्पा और अत्याचार के भेद के प्रति उदासीन 5. दुर्घटनाओं के तूफ़ान में

Saqi

Even when drunk, I am perfectly sane, O Saqi
In your jar it is not wine, it looks, but something else prithee

What kind of a drink is this, what are these times
My heart burns in fire inceassantly

Serve me something that puts this mischievous intellect to sleep
I am at this moment unable to discriminate between kindness and cruelty

By God's grace I am still not quite conscious
But I am crowded upon by tragedies already

→

छलकती है जो तेरे जाम से उस मय का क्या कहना
तिरे शादाब[1] होंठों की मगर कुछ और है साक़ी

मुझे पीने दे, पीने दे कि तेरे ज़ामे-ला' लीं में[2]
अभी कुछ और है, कुछ और है, कुछ और है साक़ी

Chhalakti hai jo tere jaam se us mai ka kya kahna
Tire shaadab hoton ki magar kuchh aur hai saqi

Mujhe pine de, pine de ki tere jaame-la' lin mein
Abhi kuchh aur hai, kuchh aur hai, kuchh aur hai saqi

---

1. तरोताज़ा 2. लाल रंग के प्याले (होंठों) में

The bubbling wine served by you is great though
The wine that oozes from your eyes is a variety

Allow me to go on drinking from your red lips, pray
For, therein some more wine, some more wine I see

फ़िक्र

नहीं हरचंद किसी गुमशुदा जन्नत की तलाश
इक न इक ख़ुल्दे-तरबनाक का[1] अमां है ज़रूर
बज़्मे-दोशीना की[2] हसरत तो नहीं है मुझको
मेरी नज़रों में कोई और शबिस्तां[3] है ज़रूर

मिट के, बर्बादे-जहां होके, सभी कुछ खोके
बात क्या है किज़ियां का[4] कोई एहसास नहीं
कारफ़र्मा[5] है कोई ताज़ा जुनूने-ता'मीर[6]
दिले-मुज़्तर[7] अभी आमाजगहे-यास नहीं[8]

ताज़ा-दम भी हूँ मगर फिर ये तक़ाज़ा क्यों है
हाथ रख दे मिरे माथे पे कोई ज़ोहरा-जबीं[9]

→

Nahin harchand kisi gumshuda jannat ki talash
Ik na ik khulde-tarabnak ka aman hai zaroor
Bazme-doshina ki hasrat to nahin hai mujhko
Meri nazaron mein koi aur shabista hai zaroor

Mit ke, barbade-jahan hoke, sabhi kuchh khoke
baat kya hai kiziyaan ka koi ahsaas nahin
Karfarma hai koi taza junune-ta'mir
Dile-muztar abhi aamajagahe-yaas nahin

Taza-dam bhi hoon magar phir ye takaza kyon hai
Haath rakh de mire mathe pe koi zohra-jabin

---

1. आनन्दमय स्वर्ग का 2. पिछली रात वाली महफ़िल की 3. शयनागार 4. हानि का 5. काम करने वाला 6. निर्माणोन्माद 7. आतुर मन 8. निराशा के लक्षित चिह्न पर नहीं पहुँचा 9. सितारे जैसे (प्रकाशमान) माथे वाली (अलौकिक सुन्दरी)

My concern

I am not looking for a lost paradise though
I certainly need a happy heaven
I crave not the last night's mehfil but surely
My eyes are set on some other bed chamber

Even though I am ruined, have lost everything
I am not mindful of my ruination,
I am fired instead by a passion to build something new
And know not the name of despair or frustration

I am bubbling with life and yet I want
The comforting hand of a beauteous one on my forehead

→

एक आग़ोशे-हसीं[1] शौक़ की[2] मे'राज[3] है क्या
क्या यही है असरे-नाला-ए-दिल-हाए-हज़ीं[4]

महवशों का[5] तरब-अंगेज़[6] तबस्सुम[7] क्या है
है तो सब कुछ ये मगर ख़्वाब-असर[8] क्यों हो जाए
हुस्न की जलवागहे-नाज़ का अफ़सूं[9] तसलीम[10]
यही क़ुर्बानगहे-अर्बाबे-नज़र[11] क्यों हो जाए

मैंने सोचा था कि दुश्वार है मंज़िल अपनी
इक हसीं बाज़ुए-सीमीं[12] का सहारा भी तो हो
दश्ते-ज़ुल्मात से[13] आख़िर को गुज़रना है मुझे
कोई रुख़्शंदा-ओ-ताबिंदा[14] सितारा भी तो हो

→

Ek aagoshe-haseen shauk ki me'raj hai kya
Kya yahi hai asare-nala-e-dil-haye-hazin

Mahvashon ka tarab-angez tabssum kya hai
Hai to sab kuchh ye magar khwab-asar kyon ho jaye
Husn ki jalwagahe-naaz ka afasoon taslim
Yahi kurbangahe-arbabe-nazar kyon ho jaye

Maine socha tha ki dushwar hai manzil apni
Ik haseen bazuye-simin ka sahara bhi to ho
Dashte-zulmat se aakhir ko guzarna hai mujhe
Koi rukhshanda-o-tabinda sitara bhi to ho

---

1. सुन्दर गोद 2. इश्क़ की 3. पराकाष्ठा 4. शोकाकुल हृदय के आर्त्तनाद का असर 5. चाँद-जैसी सुंदरियों का 6. हर्षोत्पादक 7. मुस्कराहट 8. सपने का-सा प्रभाव रखने वाला 9. जादू 10. स्वीकार 11. पारखियों का बलि-घर 12. रजत बाँह 13. अंधेरों के जंगल से 14. उज्ज्वल और प्रकाशमान

Does it mean that the lap of a peerless maiden
Is what a stricken heart ultimately needs !

Her lovely smile means a lot indeed
But how can one realize a dream
The magic of beauty is granted certainly
But why should it be regarded the ultimate achievement of the men of vision

I had thought that in order to reach my destination
The support of some lovely beauty is a must
For, as I had to pass through a forest dark
I would need the light of a glittering star, I thought

→

आग को किसने गुलिस्तां न बनाना चाहा
जल बुझे कितने ख़लील[1], आग गुलिस्तां न बनी
टूट जाना दरे-ज़िंदां का[2] तो दुश्वार न था
ख़ुद-ज़ुलैख़ा[3] ही रफ़ीक़े-महे-किन्आं न बनी

ब-ईं इन्आमे-वफ़ा[4], उफ़ ये तक़ाज़ाए-ह्यात[5]
ज़िंदगी वक़्फ़े-ग़मे-ख़ाक-नशीनां[6] कर दे
खूने-दिल की कोई क़ीमत जो नहीं है तो न हो
खूने-दिल नज़्रे-चमनबंदी-ए-दौरां[7] कर दे

Aag ko kisne gulistan na banana chaha
Jal bujhe kitne khalil, aag gulistan na bani
Toot jana dare-zindaan ka to dushwar na tha
Khud-julekha hi rafike-mahe-kinaan na bani

Ba-ien inaame-wafa, uf ye takazaye-hyat
Zindgi vakfe-game-khak-nashinaan kar de
Khoone-dil ki koi kimat jo nahi hai to na ho
Khoone-dil nazre-chamanbandi-e-dauraan kar de

---

1. इब्राहिम (पैग़म्बर) 2. कारागार के दरवाज़े का 3. मिस्र देश के बादशाह 'अज़ीज़' की स्त्री जो (सुंदरता के देवता) हज़रत यूसुफ़ पर मुग्ध हो गई थी 4. वफ़ा करने का यह पुरस्कार 5. जीवन की मांग 6. मनुष्य मात्र के दुःखों को समर्पित 7. संसार के सुंदर सुधार को समर्पित

Who would not like to turn a burning desert into a flourishing garden
The breaking of the prison door was not too difficult a task
Ah, so many Khalils have been reduced to cinder
But Zulekhan did not become a companion
Of Yussuf, the peerless one

If this is the reward for being faithful, if this is what being alive requires
Then why not dedicate our life to the downtrodden of the world
If our heart, bleeding in love has no worth
Then this blood may rather be used
For bringing a smile on the face of the earth

आज

कारफ़र्मा[1] फिर मिरा ज़ौक़े-ग़ज़ल-ख़्वानी[2] है आज
फिर नफ़स का[3] साज़ गर्मे-शो'ला-अफ़शानी है[4] आज

फिर निगाहे-शौक़ की[5] गर्मी है और रू-ए-निगार[6]
फिर अरक़-आलूद[7] इक काफ़िर की पेशानी है आज

फिर मिरे लब पर क़सीदे[8] हैं लबो-रुख़्सार के[9]
फिर किसी चेहरे पे ताबानी[10] सी ताबानी है आज

हुस्न इस दर्जा निशाते-हुस्न में[11] डूबा हुआ
अंखड़ियां बेख़ुद, शमीमे-ज़ुल्फ़[12] दीवानी है आज

लर्ज़िशे-लब में[13] शराबों-शे'र का तूफ़ान है
जुंबिशे-मिज़गां में[14] अफ़सूने-ग़ज़लख़्वानी[15] है आज

→

Karfarma phir mira zauke-ghazal-khwani hai aaj
Phir nafas ka saaz garme-sho'la-afshani hai aaj

Phir nigahe-shauk ki garmi hai aur roo-e-nigar
Phir arak-aalood ik kafir ki peshani hai aaj

Phir mire lab par kaside hain labo-rukhsar ke
Phir kisi chehre pe tabani si tabani hai aaj

Husn is darja nishate-husn mein duba hua
Ankhadiyan bekhud, shamime-zulf divani hai aaj

Larzishe-lab mein sharabon-she'r ka tufan hai
Jumbishe-mizgan mein afsoone-ghazalkhwani hai aaj

---

1. कार्यरत 2. गीत गाने की अभिरुचि 3. साँस का 4. शोले बिखेर रहा है 5. इश्क़ रूपी नज़र की 6. प्रेयसी का मुखड़ा 7. पसीना-पसीना 8. होंठों पर स्तुति गान 9. होंठों और कपोलों के 10. आभा 11. सौंदर्य की मस्ती में 12. केशों की सुगंध 13. होंठों की थरथराहट में 14. पलकों के हिलने में 15. संगीत का जादू

Today

Today, again the desire to recite a ghazal wells up
Again, sparks come out with every breath

Again, I see my beloved's face before me
Again, a journeyman is profusely sweating

Again, I am full of odes to her lips and cheeks
Again, I am face to face with a glowing face,

The beloved is overwhelmed by her own beauty
Her eyes are intoxicated; the fragrance from her hair goes wild

Poetry and wine flow from her quivering lips

→

वो नफ़स की ज़मज़मा-संजी[1] नज़र की गुफ़्तगू
सीना-ए-मासूम में[2] इक तुर्फ़ा तुग़यानी[3] है आज

वो इशारे हैं बहक जाना ही ऐने-होश है[4]
होश में रहना यक़ीनन सख़्त नादानी है आज

कश्मकश सी कश्मकश में है मज़ाके-आशिक़ी
कामरां[5] सी कामरां हर सई-ए-इम्कानी[6] है आज

हुस्न के चेहरे पे है नूरे-सदाक़त की[7] दमक
इश्क़ के सर पर कुलाहे-फ़ख्रे-इनसानी[8] है आज

शौक़ से[9] मौक़ा-शनासी[10] की तवक़्क़ो[11] भी ग़लत
मैंने उनकी शक्ल भी मुश्किल से पहचानी है आज

Wo nafas ki zamzama-sanji nazar ki guftgu
Sina-e-masoom mein ik turfa tugyani hai aaj

Wo ishare hain bahak jana hi ene-hosh hai
Hosh mein rahna yakinan sakht nadani hai aaj

Kashmkash si kashmkash mein hai mazake-aashiki
Kaamran si kaamran har sai-e-imkani hai aaj

Husn ke chehre pe hai noore-sadakat ki damak
Ishq ke sar par kulahe-fakhre-insani hai aaj

Shauk se mauka-shanasi ki tavakko bhi galat
Maine unki shakl bhi mushkil se pahchani hai aaj

---

1. साँसों का संगीत 2. सरल हृदय में 3. विचित्र बाढ़ 4. सही अर्थ में होश है 5. सफल, भाग्यवान 6. संभव चेष्टा 7. सत्य के तेज की 8. मनुष्यता के गौरव का ताज 9. इश्क़ के कारण 10. अवसर पहचानना 11. आशा

And her eyelids cast a melodious spell.
O her voluble eyes, her musical breath
And a flood swelling in her breasts—

Such are the gestures which are worth losing your senses to, today,
As remaining in senses is a folly

Every enterprise of mine looks like succeeding today
There is a glow of truth on the face of the beloved
And the crown of human dignity sits on the lover's head

Love is on the horns of a dilemma
O no, it is unfair to think of any opportunism today
For, with great difficulty I have recognized her, I must say.

बोल! अरी ओ धरती बोल!

बोल! अरी ओ धरती बोल!
राज सिंहासन डावांडोल
बादल बिजली रैन अंधियारी, दुख की मारी परजा सारी
बूढ़े-बच्चे सब दुखिया हैं, दुखिया नर हैं दुखिया नारी
बस्ती-बस्ती लूट मची है, सब बनिए हैं सब ब्योपारी
बोल! अरी ओ धरती बोल!
राज सिंहासन डावांडोल

कलजुग में जग के रखवाले, चाँदी वाले सोने वाले
देसी हों या परदेसी हों, नीले, पीले, गोरे, काले
मक्खी, भुनगे भिन-भिन करते, ढूँढ़े हैं मकड़ी के जाले
बोल! अरी ओ धरती बोल!
राज सिंहासन डावांडोल

→

Bol! ari o dharati bol!
Raj sinhasan dawandol
Badal bijali raen andhiyari, Dhukh ki mari parja sari
Budhe-bachche sab dukhiya hain, Dukhiya nar hain dukhiya nari
Basti basti loot machi hai, Sab baniye hain sab byopari
Bol! ari o dharati bol!
Raj sinhasan dawandol

Kaljug mein jag ke rakhwale, Chandi wale sone wale
Desi hon ya pardesi hon, Nile, pile, gore, kale
Makkhi, bhunge bhin-bhin karte, Dunde hain makdi ke jale
Bol! ari o dharati bol!
Raj sinhasan dawandol

Speak O Earth !

Speak O earth, let you be speaking
The throne is shaking
The dark night, the lightning flashing and the skies overcast
The young and old, the men and women, this populace vast
Groans in misery
While the trader and the shopkeeper
Loot in every town and the city
Speak O earth, let you be speaking
The throne is shaking ...

Whatever their complexion
Indians or foreigners
Are hovering around
And wearing a spider's web,
Those who have gold, those who have silver
They are the guardians of the world-
Speak up O earth, let you be speaking
The throne is shaking ...

→

क्या अफरंगी, क्या तातारी[1]*, आँख बची और बरछी मारी*
कब तक जनता की बेचैनी, कब तक जनता की बेज़ारी
कब तक सर्माए के धंधे, कब तक ये सर्मायादारी
बोल! अरी ओ धरती बोल!
राज सिंहासन डावांडोल

नामी और मशहूर नहीं हम, लेकिन क्या मज़दूर नहीं हम
धोका और मज़दूरों को दें, ऐसे तो मजबूर नहीं हम
मंज़िल अपने पांव के नीचे, मंज़िल से अब दूर नहीं हम
बोल! अरी ओ धरती बोल!
राज सिंहासन डावांडोल

→

Kya afrangi, kya tatari, Aankh bachi aur barchhi mari
Kab tak janta ki bechaini, Kab tak janta ki bezari
Kab tak sarmaye ke dhandhe, Kab tak ye sarmayadari
Bol! ari o dharati bol!
Raj sinhasan dawandol

Nami aur mashhoor nahin ham, Lekin kya majdoor nahin ham
Dhoka aur majdooron ko dein, Aaise to majboor nahin ham
Manzil apne panv ke niche, Manzil se ab door nahin ham
Bol! ari o dharati bol!
Raj sinhasan dawandol

1. तुर्किस्तान निवासी

Whether European or the Turk
They are looking for an opportunity to stab-
How long will the people be helpless?
How long will the people remain miserable?
How long will the capitalist loot
How long will capitalism rule the roost-
Speak O earth, let you be speaking
The throne is shaking ...

Though not famous or known,
We are workers,
We are not so helpless either
That we will deceive fellow workers
We are not far from our destination
In fact the destination is under our feet-
Speak O earth, let you be speaking
The earth is shaking ...

→

बोल कि तेरी ख़िदमत की है, बोल कि तेरा काम किया है
बोल कि तेरे फल खाए हैं, बोल कि तेरा दूध पिया है
बोल कि हमने हश्र[1] उठाया, बोल कि हमसे हश्र उठा है
बोल कि हमसे जागी दुनिया
बोल कि हमसे जागी धरती
बोल! अरी ओ धरती बोल!
राज सिंहासन डावांडोल

Bol ki teri khidmat ki hai, Bol ki tera kaam kiya hai
Bol ki tere phal khaye hain, Bol ki tera dudh piya hai
Bol ki hamne hashr uthaya, Bol ki hamse hashr utha hai
Bol ki hamse jagi duniya
Bol ki hamse jagi dharti
Bol! ari o dharati bol!
Raj sinhasan dawandol

1. प्रलय, तूफ़ान

Speak, for we have served you
Speak, for we have eaten your fruits
Speak, for we have drunk your milk
Speak up, we have started the revolution
Speak up; we are the cause of the revolution.
Speak O earth, let you be speaking
The throne is shaking ...

Speak up, we have roused the world
Speak you now, we have woken you up
Speak O earth, let you be speaking
The throne is shaking ...

हुस्न-ओ-इश्क़

मुझसे मत पूछ 'मिरे हुस्न में क्या रक्खा है?'
आँख से पर्दा-ए-जुल्मात[1] उठा रक्खा है
मेरी दुनिया कि मिरे ग़म से जहन्नुम-बरदोश[2]
तूने दुनिया को भी फ़िर्दौस[3] बना रक्खा है

मुझसे मत पूछ 'तिरे इश्क़ में क्या रक्खा है?'
सोज़ को साज़ के पर्दे में छुपा रक्खा है
जगमगा उठती है दुनिया-ए-तख़ैयुल[4] जिससे
दिल में वो शो'ला-ए-जांसोज़[5] दबा रक्खा है

Mujhse mat poochh 'mire husn mein kya rakkha hai?'
Aankh se parda-e-julmat utha rakkha hai
Meri duniya ki mire gam se jahannum-bardosh
Tune duniya ko bhi firdos bana rakkha hai

Mujhse mat poochh 'tire ishq mein kya rakkha hai?'
Soz ko saaz ke parde mein chhupa rakkha hai
Jagmaga uthti hai duniya-e-takhaiyul jisse
Dil mein wo sho'la-e-jansoz daba rakkha hai

---

1. अंधेरों का पर्दा 2. कंधे पर नरक लिये (नरक-समान) 3. स्वर्ग 4. कल्पनाओं की दुनिया 5. जान को जला डालने वाला शो'ला

Love and Beauty

Ask me not what your beauty is worth
It has removed the veil of darkness from the eyes
Because of my grief, my world is hell
Whereas in your world, the very heaven lies

Ask me not what your love in it has
It has covered agony with melody
You have hidden a live flame in your heart
Which illuminates a world of imaginative reality

इश्रते-तन्हाई [1]

मैं कि मयख़ाना-ए-उल्फ़त का[2] *पुराना मयख़्वार*
महफ़िले-हुस्न का इक मुतरिबे-शीरीं-गुफ़्तार[3]
माहपारों का हदफ़ ज़ोहरा-जबीनों का शिकार[4]
नग़मा-पैरा-ओ-नवासंजो-ग़ज़लख़्वां हूँ[5] *मैं*

कितने दिलकश हैं मिरे बुतख़ाना-ए-ईमां के सनम[6]
वो कलीसाओं के आहू[7] *वो ग़ज़ालाने-हरम*[8]
मैं हमा-शौक़ो-मोहब्बत[9]*, वो हमा-लुत्फ़ो-करम*[10]
मरकज़े-मरहमते-महफ़िले-खूबां[11] *हूँ मैं*

→

Main ki maikhana-e-ulfat ka purana maikhwar
Mahfile-husn ka ek mutribe-shirin-guftar
Mahparon ka hadaf zohra-jabinon ka shikar
Nagma-paira-o-navasanjo-ghazalkhwa hoon main

Kitne dilkash hain mire butkhana-e-iman ke sanam
Wo kalisaaon ke aahu wo ghazalane-haram
Main hama-shauko-mohabbat, wo hama-lutfo-karam
Markaze-marhamate-mehfil-khooban hoon main

---

1. एकान्त का सुख 2. प्रेम की मधुशाला का 3. मृदुभाषी गायक 4. चांद के टुकड़ों (सुंदरियों) का निशाना 5. गीत गा रहा हूँ 6. मेरी मान्यता के मंदिर की मूर्तियाँ (सुंदरियाँ) 7. गिरजाघरों के मृग (मृगनयनी सुंदरियाँ) 8. काबे की चारदीवारी (अंत:पुर) की मृगनयनी स्त्रियाँ 9. साकार प्रेम 10. साकार कृपा 11. सुंदरियों की महफ़िल की कृपाओं का केंद्र

Luxury of Solitude

For long I have been drinking from the taverns of love,
Have been in the hall of beauty, a singer sweet,
And a target of the shining beauties' moonlike faces
For long I have sung of love and loveliness

How lovely the idols of heart's temple
How lovely the beauties of the church and the mosque
I am a love incarnate and they, an incarnation of grace and joy
For long, I have been a centre of their attraction

मौजज़न[1] है मए-इश्रत[2] मिरे पैमानों में
यास[3] का दर्द है कमतर मेरे अफ़सानों में
कामरानी[4] है परअफ़शां[5] मिरे रूमानों[6] में
यास की[7] सअ़ी-ए-जुनूंख़ेज पे खंदां हूँ[8] मैं

मेरे अफ़कार में महताब की तलअत ग़लतां
मेरी गुफ़्तार में है सुबह की नज़हत गलतां
मेरे अशआर में है फूलों की नकहत गलतां
रूहे-गुलजार हूँ मैं जाने-गुलिस्तां हूँ मैं

लाख मजबूर हूँ में ज़ौके-खुद-आराई से
दिल है बेज़ार अब इस इश्रते-तन्हाई से
आँख मजबूर नहीं है मिरी बीनाई से
मरहमे-दर्दो ग़मे-आलमे-इनसा हूँ मैं

→

Maujzan hai maye-ishrat mire paimanon mein
Yaas ka dard hai kamtar mere afasanon mein
Kaamrani hai parafashan mire roomanon mein
Yaas ki sai-e-junoonkhej pe khanda hoon main

Mere afkaar mein mahtab ki talat galata
Meri guftaar mein hai subah ki nazhat galata
Mere ashaar mein hai foolon ki nakhat galata
Roohe-gulzar hoon main jaane-gulistan hoon main

Lakh majboor hoon main zauke-khud-aarai se
dil bezar ab is ishrate-tanhai se
aankh majboor nahin hai miri binayi se
marhame-dardon game-aalme-insaa hoon main

---

1. तरंगित 2. निराशा 3. सुख-रूपी मदिरा 4. सफलता 5. पंख फैलाए 6. प्रेम-कथाओं 7. निराशा की 8. उन्मादोत्पादक प्रयत्न पर हँसता हूँ

Lusty wine flows from my goblet
There is hardly any frustration in my story
My romances are redolent with triumphs
I laugh at the madness of despair

My creations are soaked in moonlight
My conversation conveys the piety of dawn
And full of flowers' fragrance are my verses
I am the soul, the life blood of the garden

But I am tired of praising my own self
Tired of praising the luxury of solitude
Everything around me I can see
I know the sufferings and sorrows of humanity

क्यों न चाहूँ कि हर इक हाथ में पैमाना हो
यासो-मरहूमी-ओ-मजबूरी इक अ.फ़साना हो
आम अब .फ़ैज़े-मए-ओ-साक़ी-ओ-मयखाना हो
रिंद हूँ और जिगर-गोशा-ए-रिंदा हूँ मैं

अब ये अरमां कि बदल जाए जहाँ का दस्तूर
एक-इक आँख में हो ऐश-.फ़राग़त का सरूर
एक-इक जिस्म पे हो अतलसो-कमख़्वाबों समूर
अब ये बात और है खुद चाक-गरेबां हूँ मैं

Kyon na chahoon ki har ek haath mein paimana ho
yaso-marhoomi-o-majboori ek afasana ho
aam ab faize-may-o-saki-o-maykhana ho
rind hoon aur jigar-gosha-e-rinda hoon main

Ab ye araman ki badal jaye jahaan ka dastoor
Ek-ek aankh mein ho yesh-faraagat ka saroor
Ek-ek jism pe ho atlaso-kamkhvabon samoor
Ab ye baat aur hai khud chaak-garebaan hoon main

How I wish that everybody has a drink in his hand,
Wish that deprivation, despair and helplessness were things of fiction
I wish that everybody partakes of the Saqi's generosity
For, I have the heart of drinker but I am not a drinker only

I would have the outworn social order should change now
Every eye should convey comfort and joy
And even though I may myself be clothes tattered
Everybody around me should be adequately and properly covered

मुझे जाना है इक दिन!

मुझे जाना है इक दिन बज़्मे-नाज़ से[1] आख़िर
अभी फिर दर्द टपकेगा मिरी आवाज़ से आख़िर
अभी फिर आग उट्ठेगी शिकस्ता[2] साज़ से आख़िर
मुझे जाना है इक दिन, तेरी बज़्मे-नाज़ से आख़िर

अभी तो हुस्न के पैरों पे है जब्रे-हिना-बंदी[3]
अभी है इश्क़ पर आईने-फ़र्सूदा की[4] पाबंदी
अभी हावी है अक़्लो-रूह पर झूठी ख़ुदावंदी
मुझे जाना है इक दिन, तेरी बज़्मे-नाज़ से आख़िर

अभी तह्ज़ीब अद्लो-हक़ की[5] कश्ती खे नहीं सकती
अभी ये ज़िंदगी दादे-सदाक़त दे नहीं सकती[6]
अभी इनसानियत दौलत से टक्कर ले नहीं सकती
मुझे जाना है इक दिन, तेरी बज़्मे-नाज़ से आख़िर

→

Mujhe jana hai ik din bazme-naaz se aakhir
Abhi phir dard tapkega miri aawaz se aakhir
Abhi phir aag utthegi shikasta saaz se aakhir
Mujhe jana hai ik din, teri bazme-naaz se aakhir

Abhi to husn ke pairon pe hai jabre-hina-bandi
Abhi hai ishq par aaine-farsuda ki pabandi
Abhi havi hai aklo-rooh par jhuthi khudabbandi
Mujhe jana hai ik din, teri bazme-naaz se aakhir

Abhi tahjeeb adlo-haq ki kashti khe nahin sakti
Abhi ye zindgi daade-sadakat de nahin sakti
Abhi insaniyat daulat se takkar le nahin sakti
Mujhe jana hai ik din, teri bazme-naaz se aakhir

---

1. नाज़ों भरी महफ़िल से 2. टूटे हुए 3. मेहंदी लगाने पर प्रतिबंध 4. जीर्ण व्यवस्था की 5. न्याय और सत्य की 6. सत्य की प्रशंसा नहीं कर सकती

I must leave your assembly some day

I must leave your lovely company some day
But I will produce some doleful melodies for now
My musical instrument, through broken now, will some more fire rain
But I must leave your lovely assembly some day

Just now the beauteous one cannot tie the nuptial knot
At present, love is helpless before the decrepit old order
At present, we are compelled to worship false gods
But I must leave your lovely assembly some day

As yet our civilization is not guided by justice and fair play
As yet the world can not appreciate truth and honesty
As yet man cannot overcome the power of wealth
But I must leave your lovely assembly some day

→

अभी तो कायनात[1] औहाम का[2] इक कारख़ाना है
अभी धोका हक़ीक़त[3] है, हक़ीक़त इक .फ़साना है
अभी तो ज़िंदगी को ज़िंदगी करके दिखाना है
मुझे जाना है इक दिन, तेरी बज़्मे-नाज़ से आख़िर

अभी हैं शहर की तारीक[4] गलियाँ मुंतिज़र मेरी
अभी है इक हसीं तहरीके-तूफ़ां[5] मुंतिज़र मेरी
अभी शायद है इक ज़ंजीरे-ज़िंदां[6] मुंतिज़र मेरी
मुझे जाना है इक दिन, तेरी बज़्मे-नाज़ से आख़िर

अभी तो .फ़ाक़ाकश इनसान से आँखें मिलाना है
अभी झुलसे हुए चेहरों पे अश्के-ख़ूं[7] बहाना है
अभी पामाले-जौर[8] आदम को[9] सीने से लगाना है
मुझे जाना है इक दिन, तेरी बज़्मे-नाज़ से आख़िर

→

Abhi to kaynaat auham ka ik karkhana hai
Abhi dhoka hakikat hai, hakikat ik fasana hai
Abhi to zindgi ko zindgi karke dikhana hai
Mujhe jana hai ik din, teri bazme-naaz se aakhir

Abhi hain shahar ki tareek galiyan muntizar meri
Abhi hai ik haseen tahrike-tufan muntizar meri
Abhi shayad hai ik zanjire-zindan muntizar meri
Mujhe jana hai ik din, teri bazme-naaz se aakhir

Abhi to fakakash insaan se aankhen milana hai
Abhi jhulse huye cheharon pe ashke-khoon bahana hai
Abhi pamale-jaur aadam ko sine se lagana hai
Mujhe jana hai ik din, teri bazme-naaz se aakhir

---

1. ब्रह्मांड 2. भ्रमों का 3. वास्तविकता 4. अंधेरी 5. तूफ़ान (क्रांति) का आंदोलन, 6. कारागार की ज़ंजीर 7. ख़ून के आँसू 8. अत्याचार-पीड़ित 9. मानव को

This universe is as yet operating under a delusion
Illusion is reality, reality illusion
We have yet to give life its true meaning
But I must leave your lovely assembly some day

Just now, the dark alleys of the city need me
Just now I am needed for an overhaul of the social order
Just now the bars of the prison are waiting for me
But I must leave your lovely assembly some day

As of now, I have to face the starving populace,
Have to empathise with the withered humanity
And embrace the mankind groaning under cruely
But I must leave your lovely assembly some day

→

अभी हर दुश्मने-नज़्मे-कुहन के[1] गीत गाना है
अभी हर लश्करे-ज़ुल्मत-शिकन के[2] गीत गाना है
अभी ख़ुद-सर .फ़रोशाने-वतन के गीत गाना है
मुझे जाना है इक दिन, तेरी बज़्मे-नाज़ से आख़िर

कोई दम में ह्याते-नौ का[3] फिर परचम[4] उठाता हूँ
बाईमाए-हमीयत[5] जान की बाज़ी लगाता हूँ
मैं जाऊँगा, मैं जाऊँगा, मैं जाता हूँ, मैं जाता हूँ
मुझे जाना है इक दिन तेरी बज़्मे-नाज़ से आख़िर

(1945)

Abhi har dushmane-nazme-kuhan ke geet gana hai
Abhi har lashkare-zulmat-shikan ke geet gana hai
Abhi khud-sar faroshane-vatan ke geet gana hai
Mujhe jana hai ik din, teri bazme-naaz se aakhir

Koi dam mein hyaate-nau ka phir parcham uthata hoon
Baimaye-hamiyat jaan ki bazi lagata hoon
Main jaaunga, main jaaunga, main jata hoon, main jata hoon
Mujhe jana hai ik din, teri bazme-naaz se aakhir

---

1. जीर्ण व्यवस्था के शत्रु के 2. अंधकार दूर करने वाली सेना के 3. नव जीवन का 4. पताका
5. आत्म-सम्मान की रक्षा के लिए

As yet, I have to celebrate the enemies of the cruel old order
As yet, I have to feit the forces fighting darkness
As yet, I have to sing paens to the nation's martyrs
But I must leave your as lovely assembly some day

For now, I will again be the flag-bearer of a new order
For now, I will stake my life to save my self-respect
I will go and come back, I go for now
But, I must leave your lovely assembly some day

तआरुफ़

खूब पहचान लो इसरार हूँ मैं
जिन्से-उलफ़त[1] का तलबगार हूँ मैं
इश्क-ही-इश्क है दुनिया मेरी
फ़ितना-ए-अक्ल[2] से हूँ मैं बेज़ार
ख्वाबे-इशरत[3] में हैं अरबाबे-ख़िरद[4]
और इक शायरे-बेदार[5] हूँ मैं
छेड़ती है जिसे मिजराबे-अलम[6]
साज़े-फितरत[7] का वही तार हूँ मैं
रंगे-नज़्ज़ारा[8] कुदरत मुझसे,
जान रंगीनिए-कोहसार हूँ मैं
नशा-ए-नर्गिसे-खूबां मुझसे
ग़ाज़ा-ए आरज़ो-रुखसार हूँ मैं

→

Khoob pahchan lo isaraar hoon main
Jinse-ulfat ka talabgaar hoon main
Ishq-hi-ishq hai duniya meri
Fiṭna-e-akl se hoon main bezar
khwabe-ishrat mein hain arbabe-khirad
Aur ik shayare-bedar hoon main
Chhedati hai jise mijrabe-alam
Saaze-fitrat ka vahi taar hoon main
Range-nazzara kudrat mujhse,
Jaan ranginiye-kohsar hoon main
Nasha-e-nargise-khooban mujhse
Gaza-e-aarjo-rukhsar hoon main

---

1. प्रेम लायक वस्तु 2. उपद्रवी बुद्धि 3. अक्ल रूपी शरारती बच्चा 4. अक्ल 5. जागृत शायर 6. दुनिया की मिज़राब—एक संगीत यन्त्र 7. कुदरत का साज़ 8. रंगीन/ हरे-भरे दृश्य

My introduction

Let you know me well, I am Israr
And I am buyer of a thing called love
Love pervades all my life
For I am alien to mischievous intellect
While the men of worldly wisdom lie enveloped in slumber deep
I am awake to the world around
I am a string of the musical instrument
All natural beauty inheres in and is stirred by sorrow of the world
It is I who lend colour to the green hills
And Narcissius is lovely because I am there
I am the source of glow on the maiden's cheeks
I partake of the same vice as the poets Hafiz and Khayyam did

→

ऐब जो हाफ़िज़ो-खय्याम[1] में था
हाँ कुछ. उसका भी गुनहगार हूँ मैं
रश्के-सद[2] होश है मस्ती मेरी
ऐसी मस्ती है कि हुशियार हूँ मैं...

Aib jo hafizo-khayyam mein tha
Haan kuchh uska bhi gunhgaar hoon main
Rashke-sad hosh hai masti meri
Aisi masti hai ki hushiyar hoon main...

---

1. कवि हाफ़िज़ और खय्याम 2. होशमंदों की ईर्ष्या का कारण

If life on the earth is the result of Adam's sin
I am guilty of that sin as long as I live
My intoxication is an envy of the men of senses
And in that state of intoxication I am alert

रात और रेल

फिर चली है रेल इस्टेशन से लहराती हुई
नीम-शब की[1] ख़ामुशी में ज़ेरे-लब[2] गाती हुई
डगमगाती, झूमती, सीटी बजाती, खेलती
वादी-ओ-कुहसार की[3] ठंडी हवा खाती हुई
तेज़ झोंकों में वो छम-छम का सरोदे-दिलनशीं[4]
आंधियों में मेंह बरसने की सदा[5] आती हुई
जैसे मौजों का तरन्नुम[6] जैसे जल-परियों के गीत
एक-इक लै में हज़ारों ज़मज़मे[7] गाती हुई
नौनिहालों को सुनाती मीठी-मीठी लोरियाँ
नाज़नीनों को[8] सुनहरे ख़्वाब दिखलाती हुई
ठोकरें खाकर, लचकती, गुनगुनाती, झूमती
सरख़ुशी में घुंघरुओं की ताल पर गाती हुई

→

Phir chali hai rail istation se lahraati hui
Neem-shab ki khamushi mein zere-lab gati hui
Dagmagaati, jhoomti, siti bajati, khelti
Wadi-o-kuhsaar ki thandi hawa khati hui
Tezjhonkonmeinwochham-chhamkasarode-dilnashin
Aandhiyon mein meh barasane ki sada aati hui
Jaise maujon ka tarannum jaise jal-pariyon ke geet
Ek-ik lai mein hazaron zamzame gati hui
Naunihalon ko sunati mithi-mithi loriyan
Nazninon ko sunahare khwab dikhlati hui
Thokren khakar, lachakati, gungunati, jhoomti
Sarkhushi mein ghunghruon ki taal par gati hui

---

1. आधी रात की 2. होंठों ही होंठों में 3. घाटियों और पर्वतों की 4. हृदयस्पर्शी संगीत 5. आवाज़ 6. गुंजार, संगीत 7. गीत 8. सुकुमारियों को

Night and the train

The train once again is out of the station flowing
In the silence of the midnight singing
Fluttering, shaking, whistling, playing
Inhaling the cool breeze of the hill and the valley
Producing sweet music as it negotiates the windy blast
Producing the sweet music of the waves and the nymph's song
Producing a thousand lyrics in a single go
Singing lullabies to the babes
And weaving sweet dreams to the ladies sweet
Hitting bending, humming
And singing with joy on the anklet's beat;

→

नाज़ से हर मोड़ पर खाती हुई सौ पेचो-ख़म[1]
इक दुल्हन अपनी अदा से आप शरमाती हुई
रात की तारीकियों में[2] *झिलमिलाती, काँपती*
पटरियों पर दूर तक सीमाब[3] *छलकाती हुई*
जैसे आधी रात को निकली हो इक शाही बरात
शादियानों की[4] *सदा से वज्द में*[5] *आती हुई*
मुन्तशिर करके[6] *.फ़ज़ा में जा-ब-जा चिनगारियाँ*
दामने-मौजे-हवा में[7] *फूल बरसाती हुई*
तेज़तर होती हुई मंज़िल-ब-मंज़िल दम-ब-दम
र.फ़्ता-र.फ़्ता अपना असली रूप दिखलाती हुई
सीना-ए-कुहसार पर[8] *चढ़ती हुई बेइख़्तियार*
एक नागन जिस तरह मस्ती में लहराती हुई
इक सितारा टूटकर जैसे रवां[9] *हो अर्श पर*[10]

→

Naaz se har mod par khati hui sau pecho-kham
Ik dulhan apni sada se aap sharmati hui
Raat ki tarikiyon mein jhilmilati, kampti
Patriyon par door tak simab chhalkati hui
Jaise aadhi raat ko nikali ho ik shahi barat
Shadiyanon ki sada se vajd mein aati hui
Muntshir karke faza mein ja-b-ja chingariyan
Damane-mauje-hawa mein phool barsati hui
Teztar hoti hui manzil-b-manzil dam-b-dam
Rafta-Rafta apna asali roop dikhalati hui
Sina-e-kuhsaar par chadati hui beikhtiyar
Ek nagan jis tarah masti mein lahrati hui
Ik sitara tootkar jaise rawan ho arsh par

---

1. बल 2. अंधेरों में 3. पारा 4. बाजों की 5. मस्ती में 6. बिखेरकर 7. वायु की लहरों के आंचल में 8. पर्वतों की छाती पर 9. गतिशील 10. आकाश पर

Like a bride blushing at her own movements
At every bend doing a hundred twists and turn
Flickering and glittering in the darkness of the night
Sprinkling mercury on the railway track;
Like a royal wedding procession in the middle of the night
Dancing along with the band in attendance
Spreading sparks all around, everywhere
As if showering flames from the air,
Picking up speed as it leaves one station behind the other
Gradually coming out in its true colour;
Like a snake curling up and smiling

→

रिफ़अ़ते-कुहसार से[1] मैदान में आती हुई
इक बगूले की तरह बढ़ती हुई मैदान में
जंगलों में आंधियों का ज़ोर दिखलाती हुई
याद आ जाए पुराने देवताओं का जलाल[2]
इन क़ियामत-ख़ेज़ियों के[3] साथ बल खाती हुई
एक रख़्शे-बेइनां[4] की बर्क़-रफ़्तारी के[5] साथ
ख़ंदकों को फाँदती, टीलों से कतराती हुई
मुर्ग़ज़ारों में[6] दिखाती जूए-शीरीं का[7] ख़िराम[8]
वादियों में अब्र के[9] मानिंद मंडलाती हुई
इक पहाड़ी पर दिखाती आबशारों की झलक
इक बियाबां में चिराग़े-तूर[10] दिखलाती हुई
जुस्तजू में मंज़िले-मक़सूद की दीवानावार
अपना सर धुनती, फ़ज़ा में बाल बिखराती हुई

→

Rifate-kuhsaar se maidan mein aati hui
Ik bagule ki tarah badati hui maidan mein
Jangalon mein aandhiyon ka zor dikhalati hui
Yaad aa jaye purane devataon ka jalal
In Kiyamat-khezion ke saath bal khati hui
Ek rakhshe-beina ki bark-raftari ke saath
Khandakon ko fandati, tilon se katrati hui
Murgzaron mein dikhati juye-shirin ka khiram
Wadion mein abra ke manind mandalti hui
Ek pahadi par dikhati aabsharon ki jhalak
Ik biyaban mein chirage-toor dikhalati hui
Justju mein manzile-maksood ki diwanawar
Apna sar dhunti, faza mein baal bikhrati hui

---

1. पर्वत के शिखर पर से 2. तेज़ 3. प्रलयकारियों के 4. ऐसा घोड़ा जिसके मुँह में लगाम न हो 5. बिजली की सी तेज़ी के 6. हरे-भरे जंगलों में 7. मीठे पानी की नदी का 8. मंद गति 9. बादलों के 10. तूर नामक पहाड़ पर चमकता दीपक, प्रथा है कि वहाँ हज़रत ईसा से खुदा का बिजली के संकेतों द्वारा वार्तालाप हुआ था

Effortlessly over the mountain climbing;
Like a star falling from the sky,
From the mountain height descending,
Like a whirlwind through the planes roaring
Through the forest showing its gale-like force
Leaping over the gorges, skirting hillocks
Like a sweet-water stream in the green forest, slowing down
Through the villages, like a cloud passing;
While in the wilderness, showing glimpses of light on Mount Sinai form the sky
In search of its destination like a frenzied woman with her hair spread out
Singing with enthusiasm a song immortal
While spewing fire when angry

→

छेड़ती इक वज्द के आलम में साज़े-सरमदी[1]
ग़ैज़ के आलम में[2] *मुँह से आग बरसाती हुई*
रेंगती, मुड़ती, मचलती, तिलमिलाती, हाँपती
अपने दिल की आतिशे-पिन्हां को[3] *भड़काती हुई*
ख़ुद-ब-ख़ुद रूठी हुई, बिफरी हुई, बिखरी हुई
शोरे-पैहम से[4] *दिले-गेती को*[5] *धड़काती हुई*
पुल पे दरिया के दमादम कौंदती ललकारती
अपनी इस तूफ़ान-अंगेज़ी पे इतराती हुई
पेश करती बीच नद्दी में चिराग़ां का[6] *समां*
साहिलों पर रेत के ज़र्रों को चमकाती हुई
मुँह में घुसती है सुरंगों के यकायक दौड़कर
दनदनाती, चीख़ती, चिंघाड़ती गाती हुई
आगे-आगे जुस्तजू-आमेज़[7] *नज़रें डालती*

→

Chhedati ik vajd ke aalam mein saaze-sarmadi
Gaiz ke aalam mein munh se aag barsati hui
Rengti, mudati machalati, tilmilati, hafti
Apne dil ki aatishe-pinhan ko bhadkati hui
Khud-b-khud roothi hui, bifari hui, bikhari hui
Shore-paiham se dile-geti ko dhadkati hui
Pul pe dariya ke damadam kaundti lalkarati
Apni is tufan-angezi pe itarati hui
Pesh karti beech nadi mein chiragan ka saman
Sahilon par ret ke zarron ko chamkati hui
Munh mein ghusti hai surangon ke yakayak daudkar
Dandanati, chikhti, chinghadti gati hui
Aage-aage justju-aamez nazarein dalti

---

1. अमर संगीत 2. क्रोध या प्रकोप की स्थिति में 3. निहित ज्वाला को 4. निरंतर शोर से 5. संसार के हृदय को 6. दीपमाला का 7. जिज्ञासापूर्ण

Hissing, hopping, panting
Stoking the fire in the heart
Unbending and offended, eccentric
Rattling the world with noise incessant
Leaping over the river-bridge with a challenge
Proud of its stormy speed;
Staging a scene of illumination in the middle of the stream
And lighting up sand-particles on the shore
With a bang it enters the tunnel
Racing, roaring, singing
A little scared by the dreadful sights of the night
Throwing searchlight as it goes;
Shivering like a poor man in the cold

→

शब के हैबतनाक[1] नज़्ज़ारों से घबराती हुई
एक मुजरिम की तरह सहमी हुई, सिमटी हुई
एक मुफ़लिस की तरह सर्दी में थर्राती हुई
तेज़ी-ए-रफ़्तार के सिक्के जमाती जा-ब-जा[2]
दश्तो-दर में[3] ज़िन्दगी की लहर दौड़ाती हुई
सफ़्हा-ए-दिल से[4] मिटाती अहदे-माज़ी के[5] नुक़ूश[6]
हालो-मुस्तक़बिल के[7] दिलकश ख़्वाब दिखलाती हुई
डालती बेदिस चटानों पर हिक़ारत की नज़र
कोह पर हँसती फ़लक को[8] आँख दिखलाती हुई
दामने-तारीकी-ए-शब की[9] उड़ाती धज्जियाँ
क़स्त्रे-ज़ुल्मत पर[10] मुसलसल तीर बरसाती हुई
ज़द में कोई चीज़ आ जाए तो उसको पीसकर

→

Shab ke haibatnak nazzaron se ghabrati hui
Ek mujrim ki tarah sahmi hui, simti hui
Ek muflis ki tarah sardi mein tharrati hui
Tezi-e-raftar ke sikke jamati ja-b-ja
Dashto-dar mein zindgi ki lahar daudati hui
Safha-e-dil se mitati ahade-mazi ke nukush
Halo-mustakbil ke dilkash khwab dikhlati hui
Dalti bedis chatano par hikarat ki nazar
Koh par hansti falak ko aankh dikhlati hui
Damane-tariki-e-shab ki udati dhajjiyan
Kasre-zulmat par musalsal teer barsati hui
Zad mein koi cheez aa jaye to usko piskar

---

1. भयानक 2. जगह-जगह 3. जंगलों और आबादियों में 4. हृदय-रूपी पृष्ठ पर से 5. भूतकाल के 6. चित्र 7. वर्तमान तथा भविष्य के 8. आकाश को 9. रात के अंधकार के आँचल की 10. अंधकार के महल पर

Like a criminal feeling nervous,
Leaving a stamp of its speed everywhere;
Making habitation and wilderness pulsate with life
Enveloping the scene in darkness
As also bringing new sights to light;
Erasing from the mind all signs of the past
As also bringing new sights to light
Holding out visions of the future
Looking at the poor rocks with contempt
Making fun of the mountains, throwing a challenge to the sky
Tearing into the blanket of the night, black
And piercing with arrows its dark citadel

→

इर्तिक़ा ए-ज़िन्दगी के[1] राज़ बतलाती हुई
जो'म में[2] पेशानी-ए-सहरा पे[3] ठोकर मारती
फिर सुबह-रफ़्तारियों के[4] नाज़ दिखलाती हुई
एक सरकश फ़ौज की सूरत अलम[5] खोले हुए
एक तूफ़ानी गरज के साथ दर्राती हुई
हर क़दम पर तोप की-सी घन-गरज के साथ-साथ
गोलियों की सनसनाहट की सदा आती हुई
वो हवा में सैकड़ों जंगी दुहल[6] बजते हुए
वो बिगुल की जांफ़ज़ा आवाज़ लहराती हुई
अलग़रज[7] उड़ती चली जाती है बेख़ौफ़ी-ख़तर
शायरे-आतिश-नफ़स का[8] खून खौलाती हुई

Irtika e-zindgi ke raaz batlati hui
Jo'm mein peshani-e-sahra pe thokar marti
Phir subah-raftariyon ke naaz dikhlati hui
Ek sarkash fauz ki surat alam khole hue
Ek tufani garaj ke saath darrati hui
Har kadam par top ki-si ghan-garaj ke sath-sath
Goliyon ki sansanahat ki sada aati hui
Wo hawa mein saikadon jangi duhal bajte hue
Wo bigul ki jaanfaza aawaz lahrati hui
Algaraj udti chali jati hai bekhaufi-khatar
Shaayare-aatish-nafas ka khoon khaulati hui

---

1. जीवन के विकास के 2. गर्व में 3. मरुस्थल के माथे पर 4. मंद गति के 5. पताका 6. ढोल, नक़्क़ारे 7. तात्पर्य यह कि 8. अग्नि-भाषी कवि का

Crushing underneath whatever comes its way
And revealing the secrets of progress of life
Giving a blow on the face of the desert most arrogantly
And picking up speed once again;
Like the rebel army, unfurling its flag
Thundering along all the way;
Alongwith the guns booming at every step
Spraying bullets as it goes,
Producing the beat of a thousand war-drums
Sending a cry of life in the air
In brief, flying fearlessly
Hotting up the blood of a revolutionary poet.

उनकी जश्ने--सालगिरह[1]

इक मजमा-ए-रंगी में[2] *वो घबराई हुई सी*
बैठी है अजब नाज़ से शर्माई हुई सी
आँखों में हया लब पे[3] *हँसी आई हुई सी*

होंठों पे फ़िदा[4] *रूहे-बहारे-गुलो-नसरीं*[5]
आँखों की चमक रूकशे-बज़्मे-महो-परवीं[6]
पैराहने-ज़रतार में[7] *इक पैकरे-सीमीं*[8]

लहरें सी वो लेता हुआ इक फूल का सेहरा
सेहरे में झमकता हुआ इक चाँद सा चेहरा
इक रंग सा रुख पर[9] *कभी हलका, कभी गहरा*

→

Ek majma-e-rangi mein wo ghabrai hui si
Baithi hai ajab naaz se sharmai hui si
Aankho mein haya lab pe hansi aai hui si

Honto pe fida roohe-bahare-gulo-nasarin
Aankhon ki chamak rookashe-bazme-maho-parvin
Pairahane-zartar mein ik paikare-simin

Lahrein si wo leta hua ik phool ka sehra
Sehare mein jhamakta hua ik chand sa chehra
Ik rang sa rukh par kabhi halka, kabhi gahra

---

1. वर्षगाँठ का उत्सव 2. रंगीन जनसमूह में 3. होंठों पर 4. न्योछावर 5. फूलों की बहार की आत्मा 6. चाँद-तारों की सभा को शरमाने वाली 7. सोने के तारों से बने लिबास में 8. चाँदी की प्रतिमा 9. चेहरे पर

Her birth anniversary

With shyness in her eyes, smile on her lips
Feeling a little nervous in a joyous gathering
She sits proudly, a little abashed, albeit

The sun and the moon shine in her eyes
The colour and fragrance of springs feel envious of her lips,
She looks gorgeous in an apparel with golden stripes

Her head is decked with flowers sweet
And through the flowers her moonlike face shines
Wherein a glow sometime light, sometime bright combines

→

हर साँस में अहसासे-फ़ुरावां की[1] कहानी
ख़ामोशी-ए-महजूब में[2] इक सैले-मआ़नी[3]
जज़्बात के तूफ़ां में है दोशीज़ा[4] जवानी

फ़ितरत नए जज़्बात के दर[5] खोल रही है
मीज़ाने-जवानी में[6] इसे तोल रही है
लव साकित-ओ-सामत[7] हैं, नज़र बोल रही है

सरशार[8] निगाहों में हया झूम रही है
हैं रक़्स[9] में अफ़लाक[10], ज़मीं घूम रही है
शायर की वफ़ा बढ़ के क़दम चूम रही है

→

Har saans mein ahsaase-phuravan ki kahani
Khamoshi-e-mahjoob mein ik saile-maani
Jazbaat ke tufan mein hai doshiza jawani

Fitrat naye jazbaat ke dar khol rahi hai
Mizane-jawani mein ise tol rahi hai
lav saakit-o-saamat hain, nazar bol rahi hai

Sarshar nigahon mein hya jhoom rahi hai
Hain raks mein aflaak, jamin ghoom rahi hai
Shaayar ki wafa bad ke qadam choom rahi hai

---

1. अनुभूतियों के आधिक्य की 2. संकुचित मौन में 3. अर्थों की बाढ़ 4. सुकुमार 5. दरवाज़े 6. जवानी की तराजू में 7. मौन, स्थिर 8. उन्मत्त 9. नृत्य 10. सातों आसमान

Although feelings are expressed in a simple breath
Her silence hides a thousand meanings.
The youth of the beloved arouses a million feelings.

Weighing her on the scales of youth
With her lips silent, sparkling eyes
Nature is opening new vistas for exploration;

Modesty leaps through intoxicated eyes
Heavens dance, the earth spins
And the poet's heart on her feet lies.

→

ऐ तू कि तेरे दम से मिरी ज़मज़मा-ख़्वानो[1]
हो तुझको मुबारक ये तिरी नूरे-जहानी[2]
अफ़कार से महफ़ूज़[3] *रहे तेरी जवानी*

छलके तिरी आँखों से शराब और ज़ियादा
महकें तिरे आरिज़के[4] *गुलाब और ज़ियादा*
अल्लाह करे ज़ोरे-शबाब[5] *और ज़ियादा*

E tu ki tere dam se miri zamzama-khwano
Ho tujhko mubarak ye tiri noore-jahani
Afkar se mahfooz rahe teri jawani

Chhalke tiri aankhon se sharab aur ziyada
Mahaken tire aarizke gulab aur ziyada
Allaha kare zore-shabab aur ziyada

---

1. गायन 2. संसार को प्रकाशमान करना 3. चिंताओं से सुरक्षित 4. कपोलों के 5. यौवन का ज़ोर

'My song is all because of you
Let you keep illuminating this earth, for ever
May your youth have nothing to do with care!

May your rosy cheeks some more fragrance give
May some more wine spill from your eyes bright
May heavens, your youth touch still greater height

मेहमान

आज की रात और बाक़ी है

कल तो जाना ही है सफ़र पे मुझे
ज़िन्दगी मुंतिज़र है मुँह फाड़े
ज़िन्दगी ख़ाको-खून में लथड़ी
आँख में शो'ला-हाय-तुंद[1] लिये
दो घड़ी ख़ुद को शादमां[2] कर लें
आज की रात और बाक़ी है

चलने ही को है इक समूम[3] अभी
रक़्स-फ़र्मा[4] है रूहे-बर्बादी[5]
बरबरीयत के[6] कारवानों से
ज़लज़ले में है सीना-ए-गेती[7]
ज़ौक़े-पिन्हां को[8] कामरां[9] कर लें
आज की रात और बाक़ी है

→

Aaj ki raat aur baki hai
Kal to jana hi hai safar pe mujhe
Zindgi muntizar hai munh phade
Zindgi, khako-khoon mein lathdi
Aankh mein sho'la-haye-tund liye
Do ghadi khud ko shadmaan kar lein
Aaj ki raat aur baki hai
Chalne hi ko hai ik samum abhi
Rakt-farma hai roohe-barbadi
Barbariyat ke karwanon se
Zalzale mein hai sine-e-geti
Zauke-pinhaan ko kamraan kar lein
Aaj ki raat aur baki hai

---

1. भड़कते शोले 2. आह्लादित 3. विषाक्त वायु 4. नृत्यशील 5. ध्वंस की आत्मा 6. बर्बरता के 7. संसार की छाती 8. निहित आकांक्षा को 9. सफल

The guest

Only this one night remains
Tomorrow I have to set out on my journey,
With eyes burning, besmeared in dust and blood
My life is waiting to swallow me up,
So let us please ourselves while we may
Only this one night I have to stay

A poisonous breeze is in the offing
A dance of death awaits me
The world is caught
In a barbaric storm
Let us fulfill our heart's desire
Only this one night remains

→

एक पैमाना-ए-मए-सरजोश[1]
लुत्फ़े-गुफ़्तार[2], गर्मी-ए-आग़ोश[3]
बोसे—इस दर्जा आतशीं बोसे[4]
फूँक डालें जो मेरी किश्ते-होश[5]
रूह यख़बस्ता[6] है तपां[7] कर लें
आज की रात और बाक़ी है

एक दो और सागरे-सरशार
फिर तो होना ही है मुझे हुशियार
छेड़ना ही है साजे-ज़ीस्त मुझे
आग बरसाएँगे लबे-गुफ़्तार
कुछ तबीयत तो हम खां कर लें
आज की रात और बाकी है

→

Ek paimana-e-may-sarjosh
Lutfe-guftaar, garmi-e-aagosh
Wase—is darja aatshin bose
Phoonk dalein jo meri kishte-hosh
Rooh yakhbasta hai tapaan kar lein
Aaj ki raat aur baki hai

Ek do aur sagare-sarshar
Phir toh hona hi hai mujhe hushiyar
Chhedna hi hai saaze-zist mujhe
Aag barsayenge labe-guftar
Kuchch batiyat toh ham khaan kar lein
Aaj ki raat aur baki hai

---

1. तेज शराब का प्याला 2. वार्तालाप का आनंद 3. आलिंगन की गर्मी 4. अग्निमय (गरम) चुम्बन 5. चेतना की खेती 6. ठंडी, जमी हुई 7. गर्म

O for a beaker full of bubbling wine
O the joy of discourse, the warmth of embrace
O for kisses, the warm, warm kisses
Which should burn my senses into ashes !
The spirit is cold, it needs some warmth
Only this one night remains

Let me drink a cup or two of wine
After that I have to be in my senses and resume the struggle for life
When my mouth will spout fire,
Let me prepare for that
Only this one night remains.

→

फिर कहाँ ये हसीं सुहानी रात
ये फराग़त ये कैफ़ के लम्हात
कुछ तो आसूदगी-ए-ज़ौके-निहां
कुछ तो तस्कीने-शोरिशे-जज़्बात
आज की रात जविदा कर लें
आज की रात और आज की रात

Phir kahan ye hansi suhani raat
Ye faragat ye kaif ke lamhat
Kuchh toh aasudagi-e-zauke-nihan
Kuchh toh taskine-shorishe-jazbaat
Aaj ki raat javida kar lein
Aaj ki raat aur aaj ki raat

This lovely night will not come again
This leisure, these joyous moments will not return
Let me quench my passion now
Let me satisfy my heart's desire –
Only this one night remains

आज की रात

देखना जज़्बे-मोहब्बत का[1] असर आज की रात
मेरे शाने पे है उस शोख़ का सर आज की रात
और क्या चाहिए अब ऐ दिले-मजरूह[2] तुझे
उसने देखा तो ब-अंदाज़े-दिगर[3] आज की रात
फूल क्या ख़ार[4] भी हैं आज गुलिस्तां-ब-किनार[5]
संगरेज़े[6] हैं निगाहों में गुहर[7] आज की रात
महवे-गुलगश्त[8] है ये कौन मिरे दोश-ब-दोश[9]
कहकशां[10] बन गई हर राहगुज़र आज की रात
शबनमिस्ताने-तजल्ली का[11] फुसूं[12] क्या कहिए
चाँद ने फैंक दिया रख़्ते-सफ़र[13] आज की रात
नूर ही नूर है, किस सिम्त उठाऊँ आँखें
हुस्न ही हुस्न है ताहद्दे-नज़र आज की रात
अल्ला-अल्लाह वो पेशानी-ए-सीमीं का[14] जमाल[15]
रह गई जम के सितारों की नज़र आज की रात

→

Dekhna jazbe-mohabbat ka asar aaj ki raat
Mere shane pe hai us shokh ka sar aaj ki raat
Aur kya chahiye ab E dile-majrooh tujhe
Usne dekha to b-andaaze-digar aaj ki raat
Phool kya khar bhi hain aaj gulistan-b-kinar
Sangreze hain nigahon mein guhar aaj ki raat
Mahve-gulgabt hai ye kaun mire dosh-b-dosh
kahkashaan ban gai har rahguzar aaj ki raat
Shabnamistane-tajalli ka phusun kya kahiye
Chand ne phenk diya rakhte-safar aaj ki raat
Noor hi noor hai, kis simt uthaun aankhein
Husn hi husn hai tahadde-nazar aaj ki raat
Alla-Allah wo peshani-e-simin ka jamal
Rah gai jam ke sitaron ki nazar aaj ki raat

---

1. प्रेम की भावना का 2. घायल हृदय 3. अन्य ढंग से (प्रेमपूर्वक) 4. काँटे 5. बाग़ को प्यारे 6. पत्थर के टुकड़े 7. मोती 8. पुष्प-विहार में तन्मय 9. कंधे से कंधा मिलाए हुए (साथ-साथ) 10. आकाश गंगा 11. प्रेमिका के मुखड़े का 12. जादू 13. यात्रा की सामग्री 14. रजत माथे का 15. रूप, सौंदर्य

Tonight

You can see the effect of true love tonight
The lovely damsel's head on my shoulder lies;
O my wounded heart, what else do you want
She has given a loving glance alright,
Not only the flowers, even the thorns look beautiful in the garden
And O the stones look like pearls tonight.
Who is walking shoulder to shoulder with me,
What makes my path resemble the milky way ?
My beloved's face has cast such a spell
That the moon has halted her journey to see the sight
There is light wherever you see
And till the very end of sight, it is all beauty

आरिज़े-गर्म पे[1] वो रंगे-शफ़क़ की[2] लहरें
वो मिरी शोख-निगाही का असर आज की रात
नर्गिसे-नाज़ में[3] वो नींद का हलका-सा खुमार
वो मिरे नग़माए-शीरीं का[4] असर आज की रात
नग़मा-ओ-मय का ये तूफ़ाने-तरब[5] क्या कहिए
घर मिरा बन गया 'ख़य्याम' का घर आज की रात
मेरी हर साँस पे वो उनकी तवज्जुह, क्या खूब
मेरी हर बात पे वो जुंबिशे-सर[6] आज की रात
उफ़ वो वारफ़्तगी-ए-शौक़ में[7] इक वह्मे-लतीफ़[8]
कपकपाते हुए होंठों पे नज़र आज की रात
अपनी रिफ़अत पे[9] जो नाज़ां[10] हैं तो नाज़ां ही रहें
कह दो अंजुम से[11] कि देखें न इधर आज की रात
उनके अल्ताफ़ का[12] इतना ही फ़ुसूं[13] काफ़ी है
कम है पहले से बहुत दर्दे-जिगर आज की रात

Aarize-garm pe wo range-shafak ki laharein
Wo miri shokh-nigahi ka asar aaj ki raat
Nargise-naaz mein wo neend ka halka-sa khumar
Wo mire nagmaye-shirin ka asar aaj ki raat
Nagma-o-may ka ye tufane-tarab kya kahiye
Ghar mira ban gaya 'Khayyam' ka ghar aaj ki raat
Meri har saans pe wo unki tavajjuh, kya khoob
Meri har baat pe wo jumbishe-sar aaj ki raat
Uf wo waraftagi-e-shauk mein ik wahme-lateef
Kapkapate hue honton pe nazar aaj ki raat
Apni rifat pe jo nazan hain to nazan hi rahein
Kah do anjum se ki dekhein na idhar aaj ki raat
Unke Altaaf ka itna hi phusoon kafi hai
Kam hai pahle se bahut darde-jigar aaj ki raat

---

1. गर्म कपोलों पर 2. सान्ध्य लालिमा की 3. प्रेयसी की नर्गिसी आँखों में 4. मधुर गीत का 5. हर्ष का तूफ़ान 6. सिर हिलाकर हामी भरना 7. प्रेमोन्माद में 8. सुंदर भ्रम 9. उच्चता पर 10. गर्वित 11. सितारों से 12. कृपाओं का 13. जादू

So charming is her forehead fair
That the stars have fixed their eyes there;
O my fond eyes
O the glow of evening twilight in her cheeks
O the drowsiness in her lovely eyes
O the effect of my sweet song tonight !
Poetry and wine overwhelm the atmosphere
The house has become Khayyam's house, it looks
She is mindful of every breath of mine
And nods her head at whatever I say
O my excessive love that creates such an illusory sight !
I feel her quivering lips tonight,
If the stars are proud of their glorious height, let them be
But they must not see us tonight
Her benevolence affects me so much, makes me so light
That I feel my heartache so much less tonight

अंधेरी रात का मुसाफ़िर

जवानी की अंधेरी रात है ज़ुल्मत का[1] तूफ़ां है
मिरी राहों से नूरे-माहो-अंजुम[2] तक गुरेज़ां है
ख़ुदा सोया हुआ है, अहरमन[3] महशर-बदामा[4] है
मगर मैं अपनी मंज़िल की तरफ़ बहता ही जाता हूँ

ग़मो-हिरमां[5] की यूरिश[6] है, मसाइब की[7] घटाएँ हैं
जुनूं की[8] फ़ित्नाख़ेज़ी[9], हुस्न की खूनी अदाएँ हैं
बड़ी पुरज़ोर आंधी है, बड़ी काफ़िर बलाएँ हैं
मगर मैं अपनी मंज़िल की तरफ़ बढ़ता ही जाता हूँ

फ़ज़ा में मौत के तारीक[10] साए थरथराते हैं
हवा के सर्द झोंके क़ल्ब पर[11] ख़ंजर चलाते हैं

→

Jawani ki andheri raat hai zulmat ka tufan hai
Miri raahon se noore-maho-anjum tak gurejan hai
Khuda soya hua hai, aharman mahshar-badama hai
Magar main apni manzil ki taraf bahata hi jata hoon

Gamo-hirman ki yurish hai, masaaib ki ghatayein hain
Junun ki fitnakhezi, husn ki khooni adayein hain
Badi purzor aandhi hai, badi kaafir balayein hain
Magar main apni manzil ki taraf badta hi jata hoon

Faza mein maut ke tareekh saaye thartharate hain
Hawa ke sard jhonke kalb par khanjar chalate hain

---

1. अंधकार का 2. चाँद-सितारों का प्रकाश 3. शैतान 4. प्रलय मचाए हुए 5. दुखों और निराशाओं की 6. आक्रमण 7. आपत्तियों की 8. उन्माद की 9. उपद्रव 10. काले 11. हृदय पर

Traveller of the dark night

It is the dark night of my youth and the darkness is most intense
Even the moon and stars avoid my path
Saturn is playing havoc while God in slumber lies
But I am marching ahead towards my destination

Sorrows and despair invade and misfortunes assail
My passion is at its peak while beauty is at its murderous best
The winds howl and the hurdles baffle
But I am marching ahead towards my destination

Dark shadows of death dance around
And the cold winds on the sky pierce like a sword

→

गुज़श्ता इश्रतों के[1] ख़्वाब आईना दिखाते हैं
मगर मैं अपनी मंज़िल की तरफ़ बढ़ता ही जाता हूँ

ज़मीं चीं-बर-जबीं[2] है आस्मां तख़रीब पर[3] माइल
रफ़ीक़ाने-सफ़र में कोई बिस्मिल[4] है कोई घाइल
तआ़क़ुब में लुटेरे हैं, चटाने राह में हाइल
मगर मैं अपनी मंज़िल की तरफ़ बढ़ता ही जाता हूँ

उफ़क़ पर[5] ज़िन्दगी के लश्करे-ज़ुल्मत का डेरा है
हवादिस के[6] क़ियामत-ख़ेज़ तूफ़ानों ने घेरा है
जहाँ तक देख सकता हूँ, अंधेरा ही अंधेरा है
मगर मैं अपनी मंज़िल की तरफ़ बढ़ता ही जाता हूँ

Guzashta ishraton ke khwab aaina dikhate hain
Magar main apni manzil ki taraf badta hi jata hoon

Zamin chin-bar-jabin hai aasman takhrib par maail
Rafikane-safar mein koi bismil hai koi ghaail
taakub mein lutere hain, chatane raah mein haail
Magar main apni manzil ki taraf badta hi jata hoon

Ufak par zindgi ke lashkare-zulmat ka dera hai
Hwadis ke kiyamat-khez tufanon ne ghera hai
Jahan tak dekh sakta hoon, andhera hi andhera hai
Magar main apni manzil ki taraf badth hi jata hoon

---

1. सुख भोगों के 2. माथे पर बल डाले हुए 3. विनाश पर 4. आहत 5. क्षितिज पर 6. दुर्घटनाओं के

While the memories of old pleasures haunt like a dream
But I am marching ahead towards my destination

The forehead of the earth is knit and the sky is bent upon destruction
Among the fellow-travellers, some are wounded, some injured
The robbers lie in wait and the rocks block our path
But I am marching ahead towards my destination

The forces of darkness surround the horizon
Massive tragedies have in battalions come
And there is gloom around as far as the eye can see
But I am marching ahead towards my destination

→

चिराग़े-दैर[1] *फ़ानूसे-हरम*[2] *क़ंदीले-रहबानी*[3]
ये सब हैं मुद्दतों से बेनियाज़े-नूरे-इर्फ़ानी[4]
न नाक़ूसे-बिरहमन[5] *है, न आहंगे-हुदी-ख़्वानी*[6]
मगर मैं अपनी मंज़िल की तरफ़ बढ़ता ही जाता हूँ

बदी पर बारिशे-लुत्फ़ो-करम, नेकी पे तक़्रीरें
जवानी के हसीं ख़्वाबों की हैबतनाक ता'बीरें[7]
नुकीली तेज़ संगीनें हैं ख़ूं-आशाम[8] *शमशीरें*
मगर मैं अपनी मंज़िल की तरफ़ बढ़ता ही जाता हूँ

हुकूमत के मज़ाहिर[9] *जंग के पुरहौल नक़्शे हैं*
कुदालों के मुक़ाबिल तोप बन्दूकें हैं नेज़े हैं
सलासिल[10]*, ताज़ियाने, बेड़ियाँ फाँसी के तख़्ते हैं*
मगर मैं अपनी मंज़िल की तरफ़ बढ़ता ही जाता हूँ

→

Chirage-dair fanuse-haram kandile-rahbani
Ye sab hain muddaton se beniyaze-noore-irfani
Na nakuse-birahman hai, na aahange-hudi-khwani
Magar main apni manzil ki taraf badta hi jata hoon

Badi par barishe-lutfo-karam, neki pe takriren
Jawani ke hansi khwabon ki habatnak ta'biren
Nukili tez sangine hain khoon-aasham shamshiren
Magar main apni manzil ki taraf badta hi jata hoon

Hukumat ka mazahir jang ke purhaul nakshe hain
Kudalon ke mukabil top banduken hain naize hain
salaasil, taziyane, bediyaan phansi ke takhte hain
Magar main apni manzil ki taraf badta hi jata hoon

---

1. मंदिर का दीपक 2. मस्जिद का फ़ानूस 3. गिरजाघर की मोमबत्ती 4. ब्रह्मज्ञान की ज्योति से बेपरवाह 5. ब्राह्मण के शंख (फूँकने की आवाज़) 6. (मुल्ला के) कुरान पढ़ने का आलाप 7. स्वप्न-फल 8. लहू पीने वाली 9. प्रदर्शन 10. ज़ंजीरें

Lamp of the temple, the glass shade of the candle in the mosque
And the taper in the church
Have long been divorced from divine light
There is neither the sound of Brahmins conch nor is there the recitation of Quran
But I am marching ahead towards my destination

Evil is blessed while goodness is lectured upon
Sweet dreams of youth find realization bitter
And we are beseiged by sharp, blood sucking swords
But I am marching ahead towards my destination

There are state-abetted demonstrations horrifying plans of war
The spades face guns and spears
And people are confronted with chains, whips and fetters
But I am marching ahead towards my destination

→

उफ़ुक़ पर जंग का ख़ूनी सितारा जगमगाता है
हर इक झोंका हवा का मौत का पैग़ाम लाता है
घटा की घन-गरज से क़ल्बे-गेती[1] काँप जाता है
मगर मैं अपनी मंज़िल की तरफ़ बढ़ता ही जाता हूँ

फ़ना के आहनी वहशत-असर[2] क़दमों की आहट है
धुएँ की बदलियाँ हैं गोलियों की सनसनाहट है
अजल के[3] क़हक़हे हैं ज़लज़लों की गड़गड़ाहट है
मगर मैं अपनी मंज़िल की तरफ़ बढ़ता ही जाता हूँ

Ufuq par jang ka khooni sitara jagmagata hai
Har ik jhonka hawa ka maut ka paigam lata hai
Ghata ki ghan-garaj se kalbe-geti kaanp jata hai
Magar main apni manzil ki taraf badhta hi jata hoon

Fana ke aahni wahshat-asar kadamon ki aahat hai
Dhuyein ki badliyaan hain goliyon ki sansanahat hai
Ajal ke kahkahe hain zaljalon ki gadgadahat hai
Magar main apni manzil ki taraf badta hi jata hoon

1. संसार का हृदय 2. भीषण 3. काल के

Bloody star of war blazes the horizon
Every gust of wind is a messenger of death
And humanity's heart is shaken by the howling breezes
But I am marching ahead towards my destination

The sound of approaching destruction is clearly heard
Clouds of smoke cover the sky and the bullets ring,
Death laughs aloud as the quake shakes the earth
But I am marching ahead towards my destination

नन्ही पुजारिन

इक नन्ही-मुन्नी सी 'पुजारिन
पतली बांहें, पतली गरदन
भोर भये मन्दिर आई है
आई नहीं है माँ लाई है
वक़्त से पहले जाग उठी है
नींद अभी आँखों में भरी है
ठोड़ी तक लट आई हुई है
यूँही सी लहराई हुई है
आँखों में तारों की चमक है
मुखड़े पर चाँदी की झलक है
कैसी सुन्दर है क्या कहिए
नन्ही सी इक सीता कहिए
धूप चढ़े तारा चमका है

→

Ek nanhi-munni si pujarin
Patli baahein, patli gardan
Bhor bhaye mandir aai hai
Aai nahin hai maa lai hai
Vakt se pahle jaag uthi hai
Nind abhi aankhon mein bhari hai
Thodi tak lat aai hui hai
Yunhi si lahrai hui hai
Aankhon mein taron ki chamak hai
Mukhade par chandi ki jhalak hai
Kaisi sundar hai kya kahiye
Nanhi si ik sita kahiye
Dhoop chade tara chamka hai

The little worshipper

Arms thin, her neck is slender
A little worshipper
Has come to the temple early in the morning,
Not come exactly, but has been brought
by her mother;
With her eyes still full of sleep
She has been woken up before time
Her hair reaches only up to the chin
Her face is silver-bright
Stars shine in her eyes.
What a lovely child
A little Sita one may say

→

पत्थर पर इक फूल खिला है
चाँद का टुकड़ा, फूल की डाली
कमसिन, सीधी, भोली-भाली
कान में चाँदी की बाली है
हाथ में पीतल की थाली है
दिल में लेकिन ध्यान नहीं है
पूजा का कुछ ज्ञान नहीं है
कैसी भोली और सीधी है
मन्दिर की छत देख रही है
माँ बढ़कर चुटकी लेती है
चुपके-चुपके हँस देती है
हँसना रोना उसका मज़हब
उसको पूजा से क्या मतलब
खुद तो आई है मन्दिर में
मन उसका है गुड़िया-घर में

Patthar par ik phool khila hai
Chand ka tukada, phool ki dali hai
Kamsin, sidhi, bholi-bhali
Kan mein chandi ki bali hai
Hath mein pital ki thali hai
Dil main lekin dhyan nahin hai
Pooja ka kuchh gyan nahin hai
Kaisi bholi aur sidhi hai
Mandir ki chhat dekh rahi hai
Maa badkar chutki leti hai
Chupke-chupke hans deti hai
Hansna rona uska mazhab
Usko pooja se kya matlab
Khud to aai hai mandir mein
Mann uska hai gudiya-ghar mein

Or perhaps a flower has blossomed on the rock;
Like the moon, like the rose-bough,
Simple, straight, innocent;
She has silver rings in the ear
And a brass plate in hand;
Ignorant completely about worship
She is not thinking of it
But staring at the temple ceiling instead
Her mother tickles her and gently smiles;
Crying and laughter are her religion
Least concerned with worship,
Her heart is the Doll's House doth dwell
Although she has come to the temple as well

शौक़े-गुरेज़ां[1]

दैरो-का'बा[2] का मैं नहीं क़ाइल
दैरो-का'बा को आस्तां[3] न बना
मुझमें तू रूहे-सरमदी[4] मत फूंक
रौनक़े-बज़्मे-आरिफ़ां[5] न बना
दश्ते-ज़ुल्मात में[6] भटकने दे
मेरी राहों को कहकशां[7] न बना
इश्रते-जह्लो-तीरगी[8] मत छीन
महरमे-राज़े-दो-जहां[9] न बना
बिजलियों से जहाँ न हो चश्मक[10]
उस गुलिस्तां में आशियां न बना

→

Dairo-ka'ba ka main nahin kaail
Dairo-ka'ba ko aastan na bana
Mujhmein tu roohe-sarmadi mat phoonk
Raunke-bazme-aarifan na bana
Dashte-zulmat mein bhatkane de
Meri raahon ko kahkashan na bana
Ishrate-jahlo-tiragi mat chhin
Maharame-raaze-do-jahan na bana
Bijaliyon se jahan na ho chashmak
Us gulistan mein aashiyan na bana

---

1. विरक्ति की आकांक्षा 2. मन्दिर और का'बा (मस्जिद) 3. पूजनीय चौखट, दहलीज़ 4. अनश्वर आत्मा 5. ब्रह्मज्ञानियों की सभा की शोभा 6. अंधकार (अज्ञान) के जंगल में 7. आकाश-गंगा 8. अज्ञानता का आनंद 9. दोनों लोकों के रहस्य का जानकार 10. लाग-डांट

Desire for detachment

I subscribe neither to the temple nor mosque
Let me visit them not
Let me not be a part of the seer's assembly
Bless me not with a soul immortal
Let me rather wander in the forest dark
My pathways illuminate not-
But pray deprive me not of the bliss of ignorance
Let me not know the secrets of this world or the other
Let my nest not nestle in a garden unknown to lightning

→

मेरी जानिब[1] निगाहे-लुत्फ़[2] न कर
ग़म को इस दर्जा कामरां[3] न बना
इस ज़मीं को ज़मीं ही रहने दे
इस ज़मीं को तू आस्मां न बना
राज़ तेरा छुपा नहीं सकता
मुझे तू अपना राज़दां[4] न बना

Meri jaanib nigahe-lutf na kar
Gam ko is darja kaamran na bana
Is zamin ko zamin hi rahne de
Is zamin ko tu aasaman na bana
Raaz tera chhupa nahin sakta
Mujhe tu apna raazdan na bana

---

1. ओर 2. प्यार की नज़र 3. विजयी 4. विश्वसनीय साथी

Let you not be moved by my sorrow,
Not ever a kind glance cast,
Rather than being high like the sky
Let me remain a creature of this earth only;
Make me not your confidant, pray
I cannot hide your secret, I must say

शिकवा-ए-मुख़्तसर[1]

मुझे शिकवा नहीं दुनिया की उन ज़ोहरा जबीनों से[2]
हुई जिनसे न मेरे शौक़े-रुसवा की[3] *पज़ीराई*[4]
मुझे शिकवा नहीं उन पाक-बातिन[5] *नुक्ताचीनों से*[6]
लबे-मौज्ज़िनुमा ने[7] *जिनके मुझ पर आग बरसाई*
मुझे शिकवा नहीं तहज़ीब के उन पासबानों से[8]
न लेने दी जिन्होंने फितरते-शायर को[9] *अंगड़ाई*
मुझे शिकवा नहीं दैरो-हरम के[10] *आस्तानों से*[11]
वो, जिनके दर पे[12] *की है मुद्दतों मैंने जबीं साई*[13]
मुझे शिकवा नहीं उफ़्तादग़ाने-ऐशो-इश्रत से[14]
वो, जिनको मेरे हाले-ज़ार पर[15] *अक्सर हँसी आई*

Mujhe shikwa nahin duniya ki un zohra jabinon se
Hui jinse na mere shauke-ruswa ki pazirai
Mujhe shikwa nahin un paak-baatin nuktachinon se
Labe-Maujzinuma ne jinke mujh par aag barsai
Mujhe shikwa nahin tahzib ke un paasbanon se
Na lene di jinhone fitarate-shaayar ko angdai
Mujhe shikwa nahin dairo-haram ke aastanon se
Wo, jinke dar pe ki hai muddaton maine jabin saai
Mujhe shikwa nahin uftadgane-esho-ishrat se
Wo, jinko mere haale-zaar par aksar hansi aai

---

1. संक्षिप्त शिकायत 2. सुन्दरियों से 3. बदनाम इश्क़ की 4. अंगीकृत 5. शुद्ध हृदय 6. आलोचकों से 7. बुद्धि को आश्चर्य में डालने वाले होंठों (ज़बान) ने 8. रक्षकों से 9. कवि के स्वभाव या प्रकृति को 10. मन्दिर-मस्जिद के 11. चौखटों से 12. दरवाज़े पर 13. माथा रगड़ा 14. सुख-वैभव भोगने वालों से 15. दरिद्र दशा पर

A simple complaint

I have no complaint against those beauties
Who cared not for my sincere love;
I have no complaint against those 'honest' critics
Who most astonishingly spread venom against me,
I have no complaint against those guardians of culture
Who didn't allow free play to a poet's fancy,
I have no complaints against the temples and the mosques
Where for years, I have rubbed my forehead,
I have no complaint against those living in luxury,

मुझे शिकवा नहीं उन साहबाने-जाहो सरवत से[1]
नहीं आई मिरे हिस्से में जिनकी एक भी पाई
ज़माने के निज़ामे-ज़ंग-आलूदा से[2] *शिकवा है*
क्वानीने-कुहन[3], *आईने-फ़र्सूदा से*[4] *शिकवा है*

Mujhe shikwa nahin un sahabane-jaho sarvat se
Nahin aai mire hisse mein jinki ek bhi paai
Zamane ke nizame-zang-aaluda se shikwa hai
Kwanine-kuhan, aaine-farsuda se shikwa hai

---

1. धनवानों से 2. ज़ंग लगी व्यवस्था से 3, 4. पुराने और जर्जर नियमों तथा व्यवस्था से

Who made fun of my misery,
I have no complaint against the wealthy
Who shared not a penny with. me-
But I have a complaint against the outworn system
The customs outdated and the laws rotten

नूरा (नर्स की चारागरी[1])

वो नौख़ेज़[2] 'नूरा' वो इक बिनते-मरियम[3]
वो मख़्मूर आँखें वो गेसू-ए-पुरख़म[4]
वो अर्ज़े-कलीसा की[5] इक माहपारा[6]
वो दैरो-हरम[7] के लिए इक शरारा
वो फ़िर्दौसे-मरियम[8] का इक ग़ुंचा-ए-तर[9]
वो तस्लीस की[10] दुख़्तरे-नेक-अख़्तर[11]
वो इक नर्स थी चारागर[12] जिसको कहिए
मुदावा-ए-दर्दे-जिगर[13] जिसको कहिए
जवानी से तिफ़ली[14] गले मिल रही थी
हवा चल रही थी कली खिल रही थी
वो पुररो'ब तेवर वो शादाब[15] चेहरा
मता-ए-जवानी पे[16] फ़ितरत का[17] पहरा

→

Wo naukhez 'Noora' wo ik binte-mariyam
Wo makhmoor aankhen wo gesu-e-purkham
Wo arze-kalisa ki ik maahpara
Wo dairo-haram ke liye ik sharara
Wo firdause-mariyam ka ik gunch-e-tar
Wo taslim ki dukhtare-nek-akhtar
Wo ik nurse thi charagar jisko kahiye
Mudawa-e-darde-jigar jisko kahiye
Jawani se tifali gale mil rahi thi
Hawa chal rahi thi kali khil rahi thi
Wo purro'b tevar wo shadab chehra
mataa-e-jawani pe fitrat ka pahra

---

1. उपचार 2. नवयुवा 3. मरियम की बेटी 4. पेचदार केश 5. ईसाइयों के देश की 6. चाँद का टुकड़ा 7. मंदिर, मस्जिद 8. मरियम की जन्नत 9. खिली कली 10. ईसाइयत की 11. सुपुत्री 12. उपचारक 13. हृदय की पीड़ा का इलाज 14. बाल्यावस्था 15. सुसिक्त, खिला 16. यौवन-धन पर 17. प्रकृति का

Noora

That youthful Noora, that daughter of Mary
Those intoxicated eyes, those curls in flurry.
That shining moon of Christian sky,
That flame for the temple and mosque fiery.
That blooming bud of Mary's garden
That daughter of humanity's guardian.
The nurse who could assuage the heartache all
The child who was turning a blooming youth
That caressing wind was turning her a bud so smooth.
That commanding look and that glowing face
And guarding this youthful beauty was nature's gaze.
O denizens of this earth, "I am your boss and I am your head,"

→

मिरी हुक्मरानी है अहले-ज़मीं पर[1]
ये तहरीर[2] था साफ़ उसकी जबीं पर[3]
सफ़ेद और शफ़्फ़ाफ़ कपड़े पहन कर
मिरे पास आती थी इक हूर बन कर
वो इक आस्मानी .फ़रिश्ता थी गोया
कि अन्दाज़ था उसमें 'जिबरील' का सा
वो तस्कीने-दिल थी सुकूने-नज़र थी
निगारे-शफ़क़[4] थी जमाले-सहर[5] थी
वो शो'ला, वो बिजली, वो जल्वा, वो परतौ[6]
'सुलेमां' की वो इक कनीज़े-सुबकरौ[7]
कभी उसकी शोख़ी में संजीदगी थी
कभी उसकी संजीदगी में भी शोख़ी
घड़ी चुप, घड़ी करने लगती थी बातें
सरहाने मिरे काट देती थी रातें

→

Miri hukmrani hai ahle-zamin par
Ye tehrir tha saaf uski jabin par
Safed aur shaffaf kapde pahan kar
Mire paas aati thi ik hoor ban kar
Wo ik aasmani farishta thi goya
Ki andaaz tha usmein 'Jibril' ka sa
Wo taskine-dil thi sukune-nazar thi
Nigare-shafak thi jamaale-sahar thi
Wo sho'la, wo bijli, wo jalwa, wo partau
'Suleman' ki wo ik kanije-subkarau
Kabhi uski shokhi mein sanjidagi thi
Kabhi uski sanjidagi mein bhi shokhi
Ghadi chup, Ghadi karne lagti thi baatein
Sarhane mire kaat deti thi raatein

---

1. धरती के वासियों पर 2. लिखा हुआ 3. माथे पर 4. अरुणिमा का सौंदर्य 5. प्रभात का सौंदर्य 6. प्रतिबिम्ब 7. सुलेमान बादशाह की मृदुल चाल वाली दासी

Was written clearly on her forehead.
Clad in pure and spotless white, like a fairy she would visit my bedside.
She was an angel from heavenly skies
With Gabriel's persona and his style.
She comforted my heart and soothed my eyes
She, the beauty of rosy morn and early morning skies
She was a flame, a current, a beauty and a reflection
Of the most nimble-footed maiden at king Suleiman's court.
Sometimes there was a playfulness in her seriousness
And sometimes even her seriousness became playful
Quiet for a moment, loquacious another
Near my pillow she spent one night after another,

→

अजब चीज़ थी वो, अजब राज़[1] थी वो
कभी सोज़ थी वो, कभी साज़ थी वो
नक़ाहत के आलम में[2] जब आँख उठती
नज़र मुझको आती मोहब्बत की देवी
वो इस वक़्त इक पैकरे-नूर[3] होती
तख़ैयुल की परवाज़ से[4] दूर होती
वो अंजील पढ़कर सुनाती थी मुझको
हँसाती थी मुझको, रुलाती थी मुझको
दवा अपने हाथों से मुझको पिलाती
''अब अच्छे हो'' हर रोज़ मुज़्दा[5] सुनाती
सरहाने मिरे एक दिन सर झुकाए
वो बैठी थी तकिए पे कुहनी टिकाए
ख़यालाते-पैहम में खोई हुई सी
न जागी हुई सी, न सोई हुई सी

→

Ajab cheez thi wo, ajab raaz thi wo
Kabhi soz thi wo, kabhi saaz thi wo
Nakahat ke aalam mein jab aankh uthti
Nazar mujhko aati mohabbat ki devi
Wo is vakt ik paikare-noor hoti
Takhaiyul ki parvaaz se door hoti
Wo anjeel padkar sunati mujhko
Hansati thi mujhko, rulati thi mujhko
Davaa apne hathon se mujhko pilati
"Ab achchhe ho" har roz muzda sunati
Sarhane mire ek din sar jhukaye
Wo baithi thi takiye pe kuhani tikaye
Khyalate-paiham mein khoi hui si
Na jagi hui si, na soi hui si

---

1. भेद 2. क्षीणता की स्थिति में 3. साकार प्रकाश 4. कल्पना की उड़ान से 5. शुभ समाचार

She was a wonder, she was a secret
She was a plaintive lyre and sometimes a musical instrument.
In a moment of stillness I raise my eyes
I would behold goddess of love in her guise.
She should have been stark light at this moment
Far from the flight of my imagination
She would read out the Bible to me
Infusing laughter, evoking tears in me.
She would administer medicine with her own hands
"Now you are well," she would declare to me each time the day ends.
One day she was sitting near the bed with her head a little bent
And her elbow on my pillow firmly went.
Her eyelashes would shut time and again
With a frown on her forehead restless they flickered time and again.

→

झपकती हुई बार-बार उसकी पलकें
जबीं पुरशिकन[1] बेक़रार उसकी पलकें
वो आँखों के साग़र छलकते हुए से
वो आरिज़ के[2] शो'ले भड़कते हुए से
लबों में[3] था लालो-गुहर का[4] ख़ज़ाना
नज़र आरिफ़ाना[5] अदा राहिबाना[6]
महक गेसुओं से[7] चली आ रही थी
मिरे हर नफ़स[8] में बसी जा रही थी
मुझे लेटे-लेटे शरारत की सूझी
जो सूझी भी तो किस क़ियामत की सूझी
ज़रा बढ़ के कुछ और गर्दन झुका ली
लबे-लाले-अफ़शां से[9] इक शै चुरा ली
वो शै जिसको अब क्या कहूँ क्या समझिए
बहिश्ते-जवानी का[10] तोहफ़ा समझिए

→

Jhapakti hui bar-bar uski palakein
Jabin purshikan bekarar uski palakein
Wo aankhon ke sagar chhalakte hue se
Wo aariz ke sho'le bhadakte hue se
Labon mein tha lalo-guhar ka khazana
Nazar aarifana adaa raahibana
Mehak gesuon se chali aa rahi thi
Mire har nafas mein basi ja rahi thi
Mujhe lete-lete shararat ki sujhi
Jo sujhi bhi to kis kiyamat ki sujhi
Zara bad ke kuchh aur gardan jhuka li
Labe-lale-afashan se ik shai chura li
Wo shai jisko ab kya kahoon kya samjhiye
Bahishte-jawani ka tohfa samajhiye

---

1. बल पड़ा माथा 2. कपोलों के 3. होंठों में 4. हीरे-मोतियों का 5. ब्रह्मज्ञानियों की सी 6. वैरागियों की सी 7. केशों से 8. श्वास 9. लाली बिखेरते होंठों से 10. यौवन-रूपी स्वर्ग का

Her intoxicated eyes oozing with wine
And cheeks glowing ember like.
Her lips were like a treasure of ruby and pearls
And her looks like that of a seer and manner like that of an ascetic.
A fragrance wafted through her hair
And filled in every breath that I inhale here.
I thought of an antic while lying down
And antic to turn heaven up and down.
I inched closer and bent my neck
And sealed her lips with a peck.
How do I describe this misdemeanor?
I can only call it my youthful fervor.
I felt that she'll be annoyed with me
And her in her usual aggressive self blow hot and cold on me.

→

मैं समझा था शायद बिगड़ जाएगी वो
हवाओं से लड़ती है लड़ जाएगी वो
मैं देखूँगा उसके बिफरने का आलम[1]
जवानी का ग़ुस्सा बिखरने का आलम
इधर दिल में इक शोरे-महशर बपा था[2]
मगर उस तरफ़ रंग ही दूसरा था
हँसी, और हँसी इस तरह खिलखिलाकर
कि शम्ए-हया[3] *रह गई झिलमिलाकर*
नहीं जानती है मिरा नाम तक वो
मगर भेज देती है पैग़ाम तक वो
ये पैग़ाम आते ही रहते हैं अक्सर
कि किस रोज़ आओगे बीमार होकर?

Main samjha tha shayad bigad jayegi wo
Hawayon se ladti hai lad jayegi wo
Main dekhunga uske bifarane ka aalam
Jawani ka gussa bikharne ka aalam
Idhar dil mein ik shore-mahshar bapa tha
Magar us taraf rang hi dusra tha
Hansi, aur hansi is tarah khilkhilakar
Ki shamye-haya rah gai jhilmilakar
Nahin janti hai mira naam tak wo
Magar bhej deti hai paigam tak wo
Ye paigam aate hi rahte hain aksar
Ki kis roz aayoge bimar hokar?

---

1. स्थिति 2. प्रलय का शोर हो रहा था 3. लज्जा-रूपी दीपक

I waited intently to see her lose her calm
To witness with delight youth in its most charming form.
I was smarting under the confusion of my act
But her reaction left me zapped.
She laughed and laughed and buoyed with laughter
And the virtue of coyness saluted and passed by her.
She doesn't even know my name
But sends me a message all the same.
She sends me a query now and then
When will I fall ill and meet her again.

दो क़तए

खुद को बहलाना था आख़िर ख़ुद को बहलाता रहा
मैं ब-ईं सोज़े-दरूं[1] हँसता रहा, गाता रहा
मुझ को एहसासे-फ़रेबे-रंगों-बूं[2] होता रहा
मैं मगर फिर भी फ़रेबे-रंगों-बू खाता रहा

मुझे साग़र दोबारा मिल गया है
तलातुम में[3] किनारा मिल गया है
मिरी बादा-परस्ती[4] पर न जाओ
जवानी को सहारा मिल गया है

Khud ko behlana tha aakhir khud ko behlata raha
Main ba-ien soze-daroon hansta raha, gata raha
Mujh ko ehsaase-farebe-rangon-boo hota raha
Main magar phir bhi farebe-rangon-boo khata raha

Mujhe sagar dobara mil gaya hai
Talatum mein kinara mil gaya hai
Miri bada-parasti par na jayo
Jawani ko sahara mil gaya hai

---

1. हृदय की जलन के बावजूद 2. रंग तथा सुगंध के छल की अनुभूति 3. तूफ़ान में 4. मदिरा पान

Two quatas

I would sing and smile

I had to beguile myself and I continued to beguile
Inspite of the pain in the heart I would sing and smile
I was quite conscious that this world of colour and fragrance was all a deception
But I continued to live under illusion inspite of my perception

I have got back my jug of wine
And found the shore in the midst of the storm
Do not attach too much importance to my drinking
My youth has found a prop for living.

❑❑❑